THE HOUSE IN PRAGUE

THE HOUSE IN PRAGUE

*How a Stolen House Helped an Immigrant Girl
Find Her Way Home*

Anna Nessy Perlberg

Golden Alley Press
Emmaus, Pennsylvania

Golden Alley Press
37 South 6th Street
Emmaus, Pennsylvania 18049

www.goldenalleypress.com

Golden Alley Press books may be purchased for educational, business, or sales promotional use. For information please contact the publisher.

Printed in the United States of America

The House in Prague: How a Stolen House Helped an Immigrant Girl Find Her Way Home/Anna Nessy Perlberg. -1st ed.

ISBN 978-0-9895265-4-8   *print*
ISBN 978-0-9895265-5-5   *ebook*

Cover image credits:

Front cover: "German soldiers enter Prague 1939" author unknown, (CC-PD-Mark1.0-PD Old); "Statue of Liberty" author unknown, source www.pixabay.com, (CC0)

Back cover photograph of the author:
©Ben Altman, www.benaltman.net

Cover design by Michael Sayre

This book is lovingly dedicated to our daughters,
Katherine Eve Friedberg
and
Julie Anna Farwell.
This is their story as well as mine.

And to
Robert Phillips,
without whose expertise and generous support
this book would not have been written.

CONTENTS

CONTENTS

PREFACE

From time to time, I am invited to meet with groups of sixth- or eighth-grade students in Chicago's public school system. I am asked to tell the story of my family's escape from Nazi persecution in 1939 Europe, to freedom and safety in the United States. And I am asked to describe my own confrontation with a new home, new culture, and new language, as a ten-year-old immigrant in New York City.

At first, I had doubts about the value of my doing this. How could I be of use to these students? How could young people, no more than fourteen years of age, connect with me, an octogenarian?

Yet I felt honored by the invitation and agreed to try. On the appointed day, my daughter Kate drove us to the school, and we climbed the stairs to the classroom. As we walked in and the teacher welcomed us, I saw a sea of fresh young faces and my doubts about the project returned. Then a girl in the front row said, "I like your blouse," and blushed. We smiled at each other, suddenly bonded by our own uncertainties. My self-doubts drifted away.

I told the story of my early years, of living in a house I loved in beautiful Prague, of the danger faced by my parents as a German army occupied my country, of our narrow escape and our flight to a new life in the United States.

Then came the questions. "Were you scared? Were you bullied?" One girl's question seemed particularly poignant: "Were you sorry you left your old home?"

Yes. Yes. And yes.

The students became involved. I saw the recognition in some of their faces. It was clear to me that my experiences and anxieties of long ago were being replayed at this very time by these and other new players, perhaps new immigrants not unlike my long-ago self. I answered as best I could, but left feeling that my answers were insufficient.

On a later occasion, I was invited to meet with a group of eighth graders who were studying the Holocaust. Speaking with these students, I avoided generalities and huge numbers, preferring to address them on a more personal level. Then came the questions.

One boy's question opened a door for me: "Do you know any people who survived the Holocaust?" That's when I told them about my treasured cousin, Paul Heller, who used lines of poetry to help himself survive; about my beloved Aunt Malva, who became my "second mother" when she came to live with us in New York after the war; and about Liselott, who told me, during a memorable walk through New York's Central Park, about books she was reading, about good and evil in the world, and about my skirt being too long. "What happened to her later on?" asked the boy. Another one asked, "Did you ever see your house in Prague again?" The time was too short.

I realized then that my story is a long one, with a beginning and an end, and that I wanted to tell it. This book is my answer to those students.

A Memoir in Two Parts

I have divided my story into two parts.

In Part I "The Early Years 1934-1945," I begin in the voice of my childhood self. I talk about our house in Prague, about our escape from Europe, and about arriving safely to a new life in New York, a city teeming with immigrants and prejudice. I speak of how I, a girl roughly ten years old, confronted a new culture, a new language, new ways of doing things. Of my bewilderment and anxiety.

In Part II "Remembrance and Return 1945-2012," I shift my point of view and write in retrospect, as an adult. I tell of life in wartime Prague, about the Holocaust and the lives of beloved survivors. I speak of my marriage and family, our life abroad. I tell about returning to Prague, both before and after the Velvet Revolution.

And always our house in Prague flickers in and out of the story as a kind of lodestar to guide me along the way.

In some ways, this is a personal story set in history. But in other ways, with immigration a contemporary issue in so many lives, as well as in the news of the day across the globe, my story is anything but unique. I hope this book helps to open the door to more questions, further explorations, and better understanding.

Anna Nessy Perlberg
Chicago, Illinois
May 2016

BAECHER FAMILY TREE

(abbreviated)

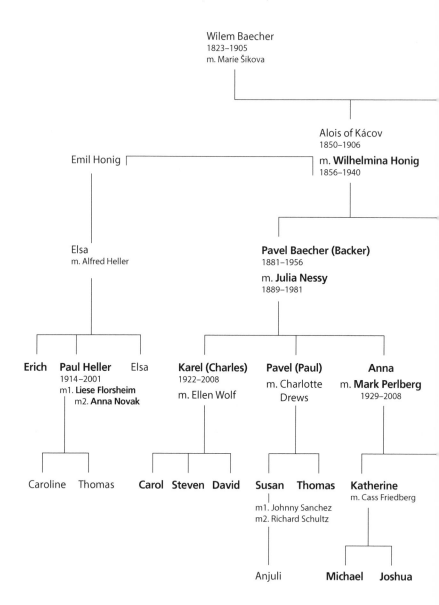

Wilem Baecher
1823–1905
m. Marie Šikova

Alois of Kácov
1850–1906

m. **Wilhelmina Honig**
1856–1940

Emil Honig

Elsa
m. Alfred Heller

Pavel Baecher (Backer)
1881–1956

m. **Julia Nessy**
1889–1981

Erich   **Paul Heller**   Elsa
1914–2001
m1. **Liese Florsheim**
m2. **Anna Novak**

Karel (Charles)
1922–2008
m. Ellen Wolf

Pavel (Paul)
m. Charlotte
Drews

Anna
m. **Mark Perlberg**
1929–2008

Caroline   Thomas

Carol   **Steven**   **David**

Susan   **Thomas**
m1. Johnny Sanchez
m2. Richard Schultz

Katherine
m. Cass Friedberg

Anjuli

Michael   **Joshua**

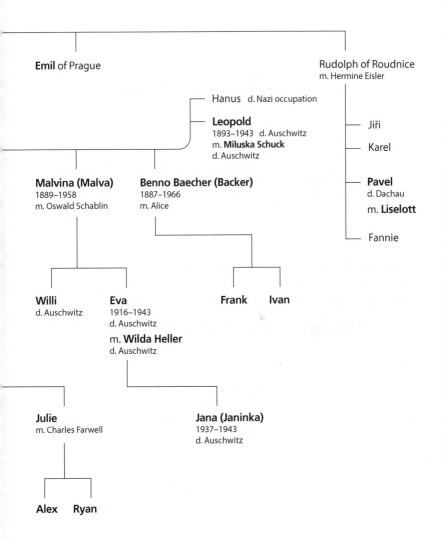

Emil of Prague

Rudolph of Roudnice
m. Hermine Eisler

Hanus   d. Nazi occupation

Leopold
1893–1943 d. Auschwitz
m. **Miluska Schuck**
d. Auschwitz

Jiři

Karel

Malvina (Malva)
1889–1958
m. Oswald Schablin

Benno Baecher (Backer)
1887–1966
m. Alice

Pavel
d. Dachau
m. **Liselott**

Fannie

Willi
d. Auschwitz

Eva
1916–1943
d. Auschwitz
m. **Wilda Heller**
d. Auschwitz

Frank   **Ivan**

Julie
m. Charles Farwell

Jana (Janinka)
1937–1943
d. Auschwitz

Alex   **Ryan**

PART ONE

The Early Years

1934–1945

The astronomical clock
Old Town Square, Prague

CHAPTER 1

THE OLD TOWN SQUARE

A skinny six-year-old girl with bandages behind my ears, I stand in Prague's Old Town Square on this spring morning. Early rain has washed the buildings until they shine – yellow, orange, olive green. Saturday is usually a school day for me, but today is special. Today we have come to see the clock.

On one side of the square I see the Baroque church of St. Nicholas; on another, the Týn Church with its two towers. My governess points to a huge monument. "Jan Hus. Remember, he founded Protestantism here, long before Luther and Calvin came along," she tells me, calling me Aničko[1] with more affection than I believe she feels.

"Yes, Miss Zemanovská. I remember."

---

1   Aničko. The Czech language is full of diminutives. Your pet dog is not simply a dog, *pes*, but a doggie, *pejsek*, unless he is a mongrel about to bite you and give you rabies. A child named Anna is called *Aninka*, *Andulka*, or, as in my case, *Anička* (pronounced *Ah*-nitch-kah). Like Latin nouns, Czech nouns have cases. *Anička* is the nominative case. If you are addressing an Anna, you use the vocative case: *Aničko*. The name is very common among Czechs.

But now it is close to the hour. People pour into the square. Café owners open their doors to offer coffee or chocolate, Malakoff pastries, and éclairs. Shopkeepers raise their awnings.

Tourists suddenly appear, led by guides holding umbrella-like signs, speaking Spanish or French. But they don't dally. Their goal, like ours, is the clock tower on the old Town Hall. We hold our breath and wait for the show to begin.

The Clock

The crowd murmurs, and I look up just as the skeleton to the right of the huge clock begins to move. He raises an hourglass and turns it upside down. He pulls a rope, and St. Peter marches out, leading the Apostles. I see a Turk nodding his head, Vanity looking in a mirror, the moneylender Greed. The rooster crows, and the clock chimes eight times.

The crowd around us begins to chatter and disperse. Tourists follow their leaders with the umbrella signs. But my eyes are still glued to the clock.

I have been here many times before, yet each time I expect something new. "More?" I whisper. I stay still, waiting for the surprise unicorn or angel to close the display. But it doesn't happen. My governess insists, "Come Aničko, we'd better start going. We'll be late."

"Yes, Miss Zemanovská," I answer, reluctantly. And we begin our walk home.

Malá Strana

Our walk is so beautiful, it wipes away my disappointment. Crossing the ancient Charles Bridge, I greet the statues of saints. Except I can't bear to look at the caged person in the base of one statue, and only look sideways at St. John of Nepomuk. I don't touch him for luck like the tourists do. Mother told me that the king punished him by throwing him off the bridge here because he wouldn't tattle what the queen told him in her confession. I don't like that story, so I make up my own.

Miss Zemanovská waits while I spin around to see Prague Castle, high on the hill that looks over our city. I always search for our house, which is near the castle, but even on my tiptoes I never quite find it.

We pass under the bridge tower and enter the Little Quarter *(Malá Strana)*, built on the hill below the castle. Now we climb through narrow cobblestone streets. We see beautiful small gardens and old houses with pictures over their front doors: two suns, three violins, a red eagle.

Finally, the top of the hill. There, at our right, is the little shop where I buy my notebooks and pencils for schoolwork. We buy my supplies, then turn right again. Across the street from the Loreta Monastery, we enter our arcade – just in time because it has begun to drizzle. We speed up to escape the rain, and the house welcomes us home.

View of the house from the Úvoz

CHAPTER 2

OUR HOUSE

Like many of the buildings in our quarter, the house where I live with my parents, two older brothers, and governess is very old. I have heard stories that some parts of Loreta Square, No. 108, may date back to the Middle Ages. Many changes have been made to it over the years.

Running to escape the rain, we duck into the first courtyard. It is small and roofed over. This is where we keep our car, a blue and gray Tatra. Father likes it because it has the motor in the back instead of the front. I like to sit here and watch our chauffeur buff it to a shine.

Two Courtyards

The second courtyard is an open square with twenty small apartments facing in on two sides. Each one has a balcony and a front door. The tenants seem invisible. Sometimes I wonder. Are they musicians like my mother? Lawyers like my father? Doctors, teachers, nurses? In spite of my questions, I never meet any of them.

The inside windows of our home make up the other two sides of the courtyard. Down on the ground floor, it takes both hands for me to open our front door. It's beautiful, made of wood, iron, and frosted glass. I tug away at it, then Miss Zemanovská and I climb up the staircase that leads to our front hall with its big fireplace. Then we walk through tall French doors and into the largest rooms of our house.

Our ceilings are very tall. Some of them are painted with frescoes which my parents discovered when they were renovating the house. I sometimes stare up at the scenes from Greek mythology, making up stories about beautiful dancers, or acrobats turning somersaults.

On this floor is the hall, the dining room, the library, my parents' bedroom, and one more room, the biggest of all. This huge room is the living room. But since it is mostly used for the performance of music, we call it the music room.

The Music Room

Two grand pianos face each other, with two concert-size harps standing between them. Both of my parents play the piano, and Mother plays the harp. But she is primarily an opera singer, and this is the room where she practices every day when she isn't on a concert tour. On those days, I like to hunker down in a corner and listen to her. Sometimes she isn't even aware I am there, the room is so big.

Between the harps in the music room is an alcove with a bay window. Standing there, I can see almost all of central

The music room

Two grand pianos

The dining room

The library

Prague: the red roofs, the gardens, the cobblestone streets, the church spires, the river. Way below I can see the steep street called the Úvoz, which our car climbs every day to bring Father home for midday dinner. When he is just under the alcove, our chauffeur gives one long beep, then two short ones. That is our signal to run to the kitchen and tell Miss Cook that Father is almost home.

Dining

My older brothers, Karel and Pavel, and I sometimes join Father and Mother in the dining room for the midday meal. The table is formally set, and before I join my parents, Miss Zemanovská supervises as I wash and change clothes. It is a special treat when Father invites me to sit to his right, which he often does.

Sometimes friends of my parents join us. When that happens, I have to dress up even more and get pokes in the ribs from the governess if I don't look polite and happy. One of Father's friends, Mr. Ptáčník, comes often. He always says the same stupid things to me, like "Here comes our honey girl!" I have to smile and respond politely or there will be another poke in my ribs.

Beside the music room and the dining room, the first floor also includes guest rooms and the kitchen. But my world is one flight up, in a group of much smaller rooms where I live with my two older brothers and Miss Zemanovská. That is where I keep my toys and my books. I love being there, in the rooms scaled to my size. And since I am often sick with ear infections, that is where I spend a lot of time reading and memorizing fairy tales.

Sickness and Recovery

For ear infections like mine, the treatment is an operation to remove part of the bone behind my ear. I have had three of these operations. After each one, it takes a long time of rest to recover and learn to walk again. My governess takes care of me, but I still have a lot of pain, and spend a lot of time alone. To help me recover, my parents sometimes send us to some sunny place in Italy or Yugoslavia. I don't like leaving my home, but my grandmother always bakes my favorite pastries and sends packages of them to sweeten my time away.

Even when I am home and well, I don't mind being alone. My brothers are five and six years older than I. They have each other for company, and aren't much interested in their little sister. So my entertainment comes from games, my own imagined stories, and my books.

School

I loved my first school. It was a private school, with the same wonderful teacher for kindergarten and first grade. He taught us to read, which made me very happy. Whenever Miss Zemanovská read to me, her boring tone let me know that she wanted to be somewhere else. So I was happy to learn to read my fairy tales to myself without waiting for her droning voice. Now that I can read on my own, I can never have enough books. One book I read over and over is a translation from English of a biography of Abraham Lincoln, who lived in a far-away place called America.

Now I go to a public school not far from our house, but I don't like it very much. The other girls are nice and I play with them sometimes, but the teachers are strict and we have to memorize a lot.

Interesting Stories

When I come home from school, I love to spend time in the kitchen, where I watch Miss Cook (I'm sure she has a real name, but that is what we have been taught to call her) chop vegetables for soup that fills the kitchen with the sweet smells of marjoram and dill. Sometimes she asks me to turn the coffee grinder for her, and she lets me lick the spoon after spreading preserves on her fruit-filled *koláčky*. Then she slides them into the huge white-tiled oven that rules over her kitchen.

If I am lucky, Miss Cook whips up a drink with cream, eggs, sugar, and vanilla for me. She worries about how skinny I am and tries to fatten me up. While I sip my drink, she tells me stories about her home village. When she was young like me, she milked the cows and collected eggs still warm from the hens. Once she took me home with her to that village and I watched her milk a cow. Then she gave me a cup of the fresh milk. It was still warm from the cow's body.

Miss Cook's aren't the only stories I hear. There are other stories, scary ones. Whenever Mother hires for the job of second maid in our house, she always makes sure it's a young girl from the countryside who knows the songs and folk stories from her home area. That is how I heard a scary story from one of our second maids, Lida.

Lida told me that one day, as darkness was setting in, she found herself near the cemetery in her village. Suddenly, she heard soft sounds. Someone was walking nearby. She hid behind a bush and saw the death figure – a skeleton wearing a black shawl over its head and a large scythe on its shoulder – shuffling slowly into the cemetery. The figure moved quietly among the graves until it disappeared. After hearing her story, I hid under my covers a bit more than usual that night.

CHAPTER 3

HOLIDAYS

Stories and drama are as important to Mother as they are to me. And there are two times a year that she goes out of her way to make especially magical for us: Christmas, and our birthdays. Even though we know just what to expect, she always manages to surprise us.

Christmas Eve

Mother loves Christmas, and she makes it a time of wonder and mystery for us all. For weeks leading up to the day, she sings the Christmas carols with us. As the day approaches, she locks the French doors to the music room, and we are forbidden to go in. She brings in helpers, but I never know what they do. Every year I try to get a peek at the giant Christmas tree being carried into the house, but I am never quite in time. I hear whispers, catch sight of secret smiles.

Finally, the time comes. It is Christmas Eve. My brothers and I huddle in the dark hall, waiting. Suddenly, the silvery tinkle of a bell, the doors of the dining room open, and we go in to dinner. On this day, I am treated as an adult.

Astonishing appetizers are passed. I make faces over crackers spread with caviar, and secretly empty my small glass of wine into a potted plant. But then – the miraculous fish soup I have waited for all year.

After the soup – baked carp, the dish that most other families in our country are also eating tonight. And finally, dessert. The most tender, flaky, and delicate apple strudel. Our stomachs are full. Now we return to the dark hall to wait for the bell to call us again.

Suddenly, the bell. The doors to the music room magically open. And there is the tree and the shine of endless whiteness, as if snow has been scattered all over it among the bright lights. Mother must have spent weeks snipping white tissue paper, wrapping hard candy in it, tying the white candies to the tree branches.

The finishing touch is always chocolate candy. One of Father's business clients is a chocolate factory which gives us wonderful figurines every Christmas – angels, the Three Kings, shepherds – all wrapped in colored tinfoil. On this day of days, I am allowed to sample as much candy as I want – and so I do, although I know I will regret it later when a night-time stomach ache wakes me up.

And then the presents. Each of us children has a space under the tree for our own gifts. What marvels! For me, it is usually books, because I love to read, and this year a beautiful doll which Mother has brought back from Paris. Now we present our gifts to our parents. It is a family rule that our gifts for Father and Mother must not be store-bought. Some years they are pictures we painted; last year I embroidered a handkerchief for Mother.

This year, Father helped me to memorize a long poem by the poet Jan Neruda as a gift for Mother. The poem is about the beauties of the Czech lands and the goodness of the Czech people. I recite it without any mistakes, and Mother thanks me with an embrace and a warm kiss.

Winter in Prague 1935

Birthdays

From morning until night, this is my special day. When I wake up, there is always a big flag outside my door announcing my new age. Mid-morning, Mother takes me to a café, where we have hot chocolate with whipped cream and an éclair. My brothers sometimes play a joke on me and tickle me to make me laugh. It is all good fun. For midday dinner, I always request my favorite meal: tender breaded veal with mashed potatoes – we call them "silk" potatoes. Father will be there, and Grandmother, who brings one of her marvelous cakes – sometimes chocolate layers with pink icing. Then gifts.

Later, we all go into the music room where Mother has set up her puppet theatre and marionettes. We all clap when she draws open the stage curtains, and there is the queen, the king, the clown, the evil magician, the prince, and the princess. When Mother's squeaky clown voice announces the name of the princess – it is always Anička – my brothers grin at me and I blush with pleasure to the tip of my toes. They find the show to be too young for them, but they sit there for my sake, and sometimes Karel, the older of the two, helps Mother manipulate the marionettes and even speak some of their voices. After the show, the theater and the puppets will mysteriously disappear into one of our many closets, waiting until their next magical appearance.[1]

---

1 Years later, my mother performed puppet stories once again – this time for her grandchildren.

Anna, Pavel, and Karel on winter holiday

CHAPTER 4

FAMILY STORIES

My parents' careers keep them very busy, so they are often away. Father's life is full of traveling and meetings, and Mother is usually either on concert tours or practicing. I don't see them as often as I wish, and I miss them terribly, but I understand this. When they are home, they show me so much attention and love. Whenever I am lonely for them, I keep myself busy reading, memorizing fairy tales, and telling stories to myself.

Julia, My Mother

Mother is a concert and opera singer. She works hard, but she also has strong ideas about how she wants us to grow up. She often says that she doesn't want us to become "stuck up little rich kids." I think this is why she took me out of the private school I loved, and sent me to the public school I don't like as much. When we spend time together, Mother tells me the stories of our family, to help me understand where I fit in.

Her father, my grandfather, was Karel Nessy, a composer

Julia Nessy, early 1920s

and organist in the church of St. Nicholas, one of Prague's great churches. He was born blind. I am named after his wife, my grandmother Anna Nessy, who lived in a village before she met him. She had a daughter, Rosa, with her first husband, who was killed in a fire. As a young widow, Grandmother Nessy came with Rosa to Prague to find work, and there she met and married Karel. My mother, Julia, was their only child.

Grandfather Nessy died of tuberculosis when Mother was only two years old, leaving my grandmother penniless, with two young daughters to raise. What did Grandmother Nessy do? She rented out rooms to students in her small apartment and washed her neighbors' laundry to put food on the table.

Grandmother Nessy brought her own mother, my great-grandmother, from the country to Prague, to live with them and help with her daughters. This was wonderful for my mother. She loved her grandmother, who taught her many

Czech folk songs. My mother sang them all, and made it her business to pass them on to my brothers and to me.

Grandmother Anna Nessy led a busy life in Prague, but she still found time to be active in politics. She was very proud to be Czech, and was part of the nationalist movement. She went to meetings and rallies, and marched for the rights of political prisoners. That's how she met Charlotte Garrigue Masaryk, the American-born wife of Thomas Masaryk, a university philosophy professor.

When Mother was still a little girl, Grandmother recognized her gift for music, so she asked my grandfather's musician friends for advice. With their help, she used her skimpy earnings to buy Mother a violin and lessons with a good teacher.

Young Julia Nessy with her violin

Mother did very well in her studies at the Music Conservatory, and started performing in public when she was still young. She studied violin, harp, and voice. Eventually she ended her violin studies and became a professional singer when she was in her early twenties. Mother kept her maiden name as her professional name, and performs as Julia Nessy in operas and on the concert stage.

Julia Nessy in the music room, 1920s

My grandmother, great-grandmother, Rosa, and Julia lived in the *Malá Strana* quarter of Prague. Nearby was the home of my grandmother's friend, Charlotte Garrigue Masaryk and her husband, Thomas Masaryk[1]. Masaryk led the Czech nationalist struggle for independence that my Grandmother Nessy supported. The Masaryks' two daughters, Alice and Olga, became special friends of Mother's from when they were all very young. The whole family loved Mother and gave her a nickname, Nesinka, based on her last name, Nessy.

---

[1]   Thomas Garrigue Masaryk (1850-1937) was the founder and first president of Czechoslovakia. Prior to World War I, he was leader of the Czech nationalist struggle for independence from Austria-Hungary. A professor of philosophy at Charles University in Prague, and steeped in history, political science, and literature, he was, above all, a humanist. He traveled widely during the War and became associated with U.S. President Woodrow Wilson. Wilson befriended Masaryk and was instrumental in the creation of Czechoslovakia in the Versailles Treaty that ended the war.

Masaryk married an American, Charlotte Garrigue, and adopted her last name as his own middle name. They had four children. Their two sons were Herbert, a modernist painter who died during the 1930s and was a friend of my father's; and Jan, who developed an international reputation. Jan served at the U.N., was Minister of Foreign Affairs of Czechoslovakia after World War II, and was murdered in 1948, probably by Soviet agents.

Masaryk and Charlotte's daughters, Alice and Olga, were friends of my mother's, though they were older than she. Alice was my godmother, and she became particularly close to my mother after both she and my family came to the United States.

The next generation of Masaryks includes the two sons of Olga, pilots who were killed fighting in World War II. The two daughters of Herbert were Anna and Herberta. After their father's death, my father, along with others, had legal responsibilities for their wellbeing. Later I was fortunate to meet Anna in Chicago, and then to visit her and Herberta with Mark in Prague. My parents remained devoted to Masaryk's tolerant and humanistic ideas throughout their lives.

Pavel, My Father

Father's name is Pavel Baecher. He grew up as a country boy in a village called Kácov,[2] not far from Prague. His parents had a grocery store there and were part of the town's small Jewish community.

Pavel Baecher, 1930s

Some Czech Jews are devoted primarily to German culture and speak German at home. Others, like the Baechers of Kácov, speak Czech with their family, love Czech music and Czech literature and, during those early years, talked about Czech independence at the dinner table. That is how Father was raised and that is why he became a strong supporter of the Czech struggle for independence from the Austrian Empire before World War I.

Father was both intelligent and musically gifted. His parents sent him to live with his wealthy Uncle Emil in Prague,

2   (pronounced *kah*-tzoff)

so he could get a better education. He studied law at Charles University and piano at the Prague Conservatory, both at the same time. When it came time to choose between the two, it wasn't easy. In the end he chose law, and became very successful at it. But music remained very important in his life. He accompanies Mother sometimes, in our music room at home, but also in concerts. I love to hear them making music together.

Pavel and Julia before a concert, Paris, early 1920s

Father made a lot of friends at Charles University, including a group of modernist painters. One of the painters was Herbert, the older son of Thomas Masaryk. Father often visited the Masaryks' home, so it was inevitable that he and Julia would meet.

As Mother tells the story, she arrived one day at the Masaryk home to visit the Masaryk daughters Alice and Olga, and heard someone playing a Schumann piece called "The Prophet Bird" beautifully on the piano. When she asked about the pianist, it was, of course, Father. It wasn't long before they fell in love.

They were married in 1914, not long after they met. The difference in their religious origins – Mother's Catholic, Father's Jewish – meant nothing to them. The judge who married them was interested in knowing more about Mother's last name, Nessy. He said that her father, Karel Nessy, had been his friend years ago. After the ceremony, the judge asked them to wait while he went in the back room and rummaged through his files. Back he came with a sheet of music – a song composed by Mother's very own father. He gave it to my parents as a wedding present.

Pavel and Julia's wedding, 1914

Julia Nessy and baby Anna, 1928

Pavel Baecher with Anna, Karel, Pavel, and Uncle Emil, 1931

CHAPTER 5

SPECIAL VISITORS, COUNTRY SUMMERS

From all that I'm told, my parents' careers are flourishing. One of my father's biggest cases involved the closing of the estate of a major Hungarian art collector named Pálffy. Father's fees were paid in paintings by some well-known artists of the past. They now hang in our home.

One very large painting hangs over our couch in the music room. There are three beggar boys crouching in a corner of the painting. I often think about those boys. Are they ashamed? Are they hungry?

There is another painting I often look at. It's the picture of a young man that hangs over one of the pianos in the music room. He looks very proud, very sure of himself. I look at it and wonder, what is he thinking about?[1] My favorite among

---

1   The painting was *Portrait of a Gentleman* by Pierre Mignard, a 17th century French portraitist. It now hangs in the National Gallery of Prague, marked with a card, "Gift of JUDr Pavel Baecher." Mark and I had opportunity to visit the painting in Prague, at which time the curator told us they consider it to be the centerpiece of their French collection. They expressed

Father's clients used to be the chocolate factory. But the paintings are better. They set my imagination to work, and never give me a stomach ache at night.

I think that the work Father values the most is handling cases for the Masaryk family. When his painter friend Herbert Masaryk died in 1915, when he was only 34 years old, Father was one of the lawyers put in charge of the financial security of Herbert's widow and two daughters, Anna and Herberta. He does a very careful job of overseeing their affairs.

Mother's career is very successful as well. She appears in operas and on concert stages in Paris, Dresden, Vienna, and the Salzburg Festival. I love learning about her operas and the composers whose music she sings. I have met some of them in our home.

Mother specializes in singing music by Mozart, Rossini, Bach, and some composers who are writing contemporary music. She has perfect pitch, so Arnold Schoenberg and his pupil,

Julia as Rosina in
The Barber of Seville

Alban Berg, use her to sing some of their difficult twelve-tone compositions. She studied with both of them, and they have become her friends. A photograph of Alban Berg, inscribed to

their gratitude to us for not suing the Gallery for the return of the painting.

Mother, is in my parents' bedroom. He sits at a piano, under a portrait of Arnold Schoenberg, his teacher.

I have never heard Mother sing on stage,[2] but I love going into her closet to finger the white, lavender, and deep purple satin gowns she wears when performing. Mother is quite short, and she wants to appear as tall as possible when she is on the stage. So her high-heeled shoes are important to her, and she has a separate closet just for them. I love to look at them, and sometimes I get away with parading around in them.

Family and Social Life

Our house is always full of guests – many of them are famous people and distinguished musicians. Mother and Josef Suk, an accomplished composer and Dvořák's son-in-law, performed concerts together and were close friends. I think he was my friend, too. When I was about five years old, on one of his visits he brought her a recording of a march he had just composed for an upcoming festival of the Sokols.[3] As the music started up, he took my hand and the two of us

---

2   There were no commercial recordings of Mother singing of which I am aware. But years later, my brother Charles found a small disk among her things – an experimental recording of her singing two Czech folk songs – which he played for my husband and me. Despite the murmur and hiss of its primitive technology, the crystalline soprano of Mother's young years came through. I was deeply moved to hear her youthful voice because by the time I heard the recording, she was a very old lady.

3   The Czech national athletic association.

marched around the perimeter of our music room. Looking up at him, I saw that we were both smiling ear to ear.

On one great occasion, President Masaryk came to visit us. My parents had a silver tea service created just for the event. And when I was still a newborn baby, Dr. Albert Schweitzer, who was making a tour of Europe to raise funds for his hospital in Africa, was my parents' honored guest. He was a hero to Mother because of his humanitarian work and his love and compassion for animals. He and Mother performed in a joint Bach concert. It was a concert that almost didn't happen, and Mother loves to tell the story.

She had learned that Dr. Schweitzer, who was German, planned to make an appearance at one of Prague's famous German concert halls. What about the Czech audiences? Sure, they could join the German audiences, but why couldn't he come to Prague's great Czech concert halls as well? She was outraged. It was impossible to her that her hero would not be heard by his Czech admirers as well as the Germans. She called to ask for an appointment with President Masaryk. It was granted, and when the time came she stormed into the President's office to demand that Czech audiences also have the privilege of hearing this great Bach scholar. Of course he agreed. He gave Mother authority to give his personal invitation to Dr. Schweitzer to give a concert in Smetana Hall – a beautiful setting where she herself had performed many times.

Next, Mother went to see Dr. Schweitzer at his hotel. She delivered President Masaryk's invitation; Dr. Schweitzer, who knew of Mother's reputation, responded with the idea of a joint concert. So that is what they did. Dr. Schweitzer played

Bach on the organ in one half of the concert, Mother sang arias from Bach cantatas in the other half. To commemorate the occasion, he gave her a copy of his book on Bach, inscribed: *To Mme Nessy-Bacher, in friendly remembrance of our concert in Prague, on August 12, 1928, Albert Schweitzer*. Below, he added, *und auf Wiedersehen* (and to a future meeting).

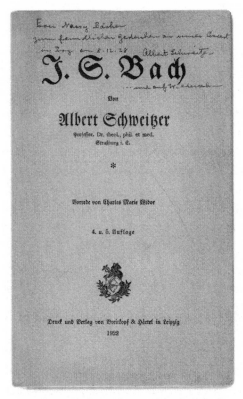

Title page to Albert Schweitzer's book on Bach inscribed to Frau Nessy Bächer

Kácov Summers

Our summer vacations are magical. Our parents take short breaks from their careers for this family time, but my brothers and I spend the whole summer with our grandmother, Wilhelmina Baecher, in Father's home village of Kácov. Every year we take the three hour drive there over bumpy, unpaved roads.

During the winter, Grandmother lives in an apartment near us in Prague. But the home she loves most is the Kácov farmhouse, where all of her children were born and raised, in the village where she had helped in her in-laws' grocery store as a young bride.

Father also loves the Kácov house, and has enjoyed remodeling and making improvements to it over the years. The beautiful and very large garden is his special project. It stretches all the way from the house to the Sázava River that borders the village. The garden includes a large glass greenhouse, two gazebos, several beehives, and lots of raspberry

The gardens at Kácov

bushes. And of course there are flowers everywhere, including roses, which stretch in garlands along both sides of all the garden paths. A very tall man whom we call Mr. Gardener presides over it all.

All year I look forward to my time in Kácov with Grandmother. She makes daisy crowns for me and we paint and play games. When I was little, she would act out fairy tales with me. I would usually be the princess, and she the young prince. Sometimes we took turns being the boy who seemed simple but was really wise. He always turned out to be the hero who discovered the secret that saved the kingdom.

Grandmother Baecher, Anna, and Julia

Sometimes Grandmother would play with me in the sandbox that Father had built in one corner of the garden. It was filled with toys just for me, but my favorite toy was the large live

Anna and her baby buggy at Kácov

tortoise that lived near the sandpile. I would look for him as soon as we arrived every summer; every year he seemed a bit bigger. When I was very small, I liked sitting gingerly on top of him, and together we would "ride" down the garden paths.

Baby Anna and her brothers at Kácov, 1928

I still love playing in the huge, rose-filled garden. I love to hide and read in the gazebos, inspect the seedlings and orchids in the greenhouse, visit the bees in the beehives, and take delicious rambles in the raspberry thicket.

The most fun times are when my parents join us in the country. Father is a swimming enthusiast, and he taught me the breaststroke so we can be swimming partners. We leave our house in our swimsuits and walk barefoot, hand-in-hand, across the little town square to swim in the Sázava River.

My parents love bringing visitors to Kácov; often they are aunts, uncles, and cousins. One of the best summer visitors

Anna and Julia at Kácov

was my cousin Mininka. Even though she is my brothers' age, she spent most of her time with me, painting wonderful watercolor pictures of the garden. Sometimes she illustrated my fairy tales for me. I cried when she left.

Summer Music

My parents' musician friends also visit us in Kácov. When they come, music pours out of the house at all hours. One visitor I especially love is Mother's American singing coach, Sidney Dietsch, who I call Uncle Sidney. He vacations in Europe every summer, and stops by Kácov to work with Mother and relax. If she is in Prague, he goes there, but I like it best when he comes to our country home. Since I know only Czech and a few German phrases, and he speaks English and some German, but no Czech, we communicate in our own funny version of garbled German.

There is another kind of music in Kácov that I hear nowhere else. The street in front of our house leads to the village cemetery, so all of the funerals pass by our door. Sometimes through the open windows we hear mournful sounds from far off, and I run to the living room window to watch.

As the sounds come nearer, I see the funeral procession. First comes the priest in his fine vestments, carrying a cross. His altar boys follow, then the coffin on a horse-drawn carriage. The white horses and carriage are decorated with flowers. If the coffin is on a truck, we know that the family is too poor to rent the funeral carriage and white horses. Behind the coffin marches the widow or widower and the bereaved family. Their friends and the townspeople follow. After a space comes the little brass band that brought me to the window, playing a sorrowful tune that sets the rhythm for the mourners' march. Sometimes I imagine the death figure from our maid Lida's story slowly walking at the end, escorting the funeral procession.

CHAPTER 6

CONFUSION AND FEAR

Life at home seems normal enough, but there are changes. Our meals in the dining room are not as lively. There is less joking with me and my brothers. My parents' conversations constantly refer to places like Austria, Sudeten, Germany. I hear names of people who are new to me: Hitler, Chamberlain. There is anxiety in the air.

The Rise of Nazism

Although the details are beyond me, I begin to understand that the source of the anxiety is developing in the powerful country next door to us – Germany. The Nazi Party is rising, somehow threatening our peace.

Listening carefully, I learn that the name Hitler belongs to the leader of the Nazis. That there is something called racism in the world, and that Hitler believes his race is superior to everyone else's. That he has written a book, *Mein Kampf*, in which he declares that two evils in the world must be destroyed: communism and Judaism. That he believes Germany needs more land, which it will get by defeating Slavic people like us, the Poles, the Russians, and others to the east. That our friends France and England do not seem to be taking his ambitions seriously. When Austria is forced to join Germany, I hear my parents speak indignantly about the fate of the defeated Austrian head of state.[1]

The Brown Ocean

It is spring, 1938, and Mother has a concert scheduled in Dresden. She does not want to travel to Nazi Germany, but she can't cancel the event. Instead, she and Father decide to travel together, and to take me along. It is a difficult decision for them. But they have dismissed my governess now that I am ten years old, and they decide it is safer for me to travel

---

1   Once Hitler had assumed total power in Germany in 1934, his first aggressive venture was to order the German army to march into the Rhineland region, in violation of the 1919 Versailles Treaty that had ended World War I. The treaty had required that the western bank of the Rhine River, called the Rhineland, be demilitarized under international supervision.

As the German army marched into the Rhineland, Hitler instructed his generals to retreat if the French put up resistance. But the French did not resist. As a result, the Rhineland became militarized German territory, and Hitler felt encouraged to proceed with further aggression.

Next was Austria, where Hitler had many devoted followers. The language of the Austrians is German; indeed, Hitler himself was Austrian by birth. In February, 1938, he demanded that the Austrian chancellor satisfy the demands of the Austrian Nazis and join Austria to Germany. When the chancellor refused, he was forced to resign and was replaced by a Nazi leader who invited Hitler's army to march in. They did so, without firing a single shot.

with them than to be left in the care of the household staff. Traveling with my parents is a rare treat, so I am excited. But that feeling is a little spoiled as I sense my parents' grim attitude toward the trip.

We take a train to Dresden, then a taxi to our hotel. Looking out the car window, I see huge flags with designs I do not recognize attached to almost every building. Father explains that they are swastikas, symbols of the Nazis. I watch the people as we drive by – many of them in uniforms, all with grim expressions, no children running or skipping.

We ride in silence. When we reach our hotel, we eat a quick supper and go up to our room. The hotel staff has set up a hammock for me to sleep in. I sleep in a hammock like this in Kácov, so I am comfortable and fall asleep almost immediately.

While I sleep, Mother and her accompanist make their way to the concert hall. I see her in my imagination: slight, beautiful, wearing her long white satin gown and white high heels. The centerpiece of her program is to be a song cycle, Schubert's *Die Winterreise* ("The Winter Journey"). She is a little nervous, but expects the welcome and success she usually receives. But this time, the reality is different.

Stepping onto the stage, Mother sees her audience for the first time: row upon row of uniformed German officers, all men. Instead of welcoming applause, blank stares. She feels rejected before she sings a single note, and relief when the concert ends.

My parents are in a hurry to return to Prague the next morning. As we pack, a low buzz comes in the windows from the street below. It grows louder and louder until it seems to come from everywhere. Leaning out of the windows, we see long lines of young men in brown shorts and shirts, singing and marching down every street toward our hotel. I catch my breath. Are they coming for us?

"Who are they?" I ask.

Father pauses, then replies: "The Hitler Youth. They're marching toward a stadium outside the city, where they'll have a big celebration. Hitler may come, too."

Finally, the sound stops. "They must have arrived," Father says.

But now comes an even more frightening sound. It sounds like a monster dog is barking throughout the city. The barks turn into shrieks, and the crowd yells, "*Sieg Heil! Sieg Heil!*

"That is Hitler," Father says. "He is addressing the crowd. The crowd is answering him with cheers." He points out the window. "See, there are loud speakers at every street corner. That's why the sound is so overpowering."

We finish packing, and return home. Mother and I both have nightmares that night. In my dream I am drowning in a brown ocean. Mother doesn't tell me hers.

That night, Father decides we must leave Europe.

Changes in the House

Overnight, life changes. Mother stops touring. Father becomes grim. He travels less and spends many days at home, often with his secretary nearby. Interesting people still come and go, but now there is less music, more serious conversation at our dining room table.

Without a governess to keep me upstairs all day, I leave my books and games behind and spend as much time with the adults as I can. Father says I have "big ears," and he is right. I think he likes this about me. Even when other children come to visit, I prefer to sit with the grownups, listening.

When I ask Mother to explain these conversations to me, she sends me to Father. He will do a better job of explaining, she says, because of his deep understanding of world events. And she is right. Sometimes my brothers join in with questions of their own. Father patiently takes time to answer us, but I think there are some things he isn't telling us.

Our Turn: The Munich Appeasement

On our walks in the city, I notice young men dressed in a kind of uniform, leather short pants *(lederhosen)* and white knee socks. Father says they are Nazi sympathizers from the Sudeten region, and a threat to our country's independence.

Back home after such a walk, we see Father in the dining room, a map spread out on the table before him. Paul starts to ask questions. Father points to the Sudeten region, running along Czechoslovakia's southern and western border. It contains the country's strongest defense lines as well as most of its munitions factories. Without the Sudeten, Father says, our country would be defenseless. The area is also a natural target for Hitler because of its large German minority, some of whom are Nazi loyalists, like the men in *lederhosen* whom I had seen on my walks. Their leader is a man named Kurt Henlein, who complains ever more forcefully about the "terrible treatment" of the Sudeten Germans by the Czech government.

To be fair, Father concedes that some discrimination does exist against the Sudeten Germans – for example, government contracts in the area are often awarded to Czechs first, rather than to Germans – but nowhere near the outraged claims of Henlein and Hitler. The German minority has decent schools, social services, and free media, as guaranteed in the Czech Constitution.

Father has full respect for President Beneš and the way he has tried to correct some of the discrimination. But Hitler is not interested in accommodations. Instead, he and Henlein make ever-increasing demands that cannot be satisfied.

Although Father's history lessons are a bit overwhelming, I prefer grappling with them to being sheltered like a child. Conversations with maps spread out on the dining room table are less frightening than letting my imagination run unchecked.

It is not long before Father's grim predictions of our coming defeat are accurate. Soon, indeed, it is our turn. While Hitler demands that the Sudeten be ceded to Germany, the British government, under Prime Minister Neville Chamberlain, wants to avoid confrontation with Hitler at any cost. It prefers to ignore the post-World War I alliances, in which the French and the British had promised to safeguard Czech borders.

And so, on Chamberlain's initiative, an international conference is called to resolve the Sudeten problem. The conference is to meet in Munich on September 29th. The participants are to be Chamberlain, French Premier Édouard Daladier, Hitler, and the Italian dictator, Benito Mussolini. Representatives of the Czech government are not invited.

Increasing Trouble

As events escalate, everyone expects that the German air force will soon begin bombing. The Czech army is mobilized. Like many others, my parents decide that we must leave Prague. We begin packing for the trip to our country home in Kácov. Mother, Father, Karel, Pavel, and I climb into the car, and our chauffeur drives us over the familiar roads. Other relatives and several friends agree to join us at the house.

On the evening of September 29, 1938, everyone sits around the large brown radio in our Kácov living room, waiting to hear the outcome of the Munich Conference. I hunch down on the floor beside Mother's chair. For fear of bombing, there are no electric lights. The candlelight makes shadows that flicker on the walls of the silent room.

Finally the announcement comes: Hitler has won. France and Britain have agreed that the Sudeten will become part of Germany in exchange for Hitler's promise to respect Czech independence. I hear sounds of shock and someone's sob. Everyone knows that Hitler's promises are hollow.

Staying Behind

Within a few days of the Munich capitulation, most of our family and friends leave Kácov. My parents decide to leave me behind, probably to protect me from the chaos they expect back in Prague. They send me to the Kácov village school, where I do not know any of the other children. I am lonely and unhappy.

Finally, the call comes. I am to return to Prague. At least I will be with my parents.

CHAPTER 7

LEAVING

The Prague I am brought back to in the spring of 1939 seems like a different city. Nazi swastika flags everywhere, German uniforms in the streets. I am taken to the city's center only twice – once to see a doctor, and once to shop for clothes because Mother needs me to try them on for size. The only people I see in the sidewalk cafés are German soldiers and officers. It is as if the people of Prague have vanished.

And now I don't see Father at all, not even in the evenings. Instead, strangers sit down to supper with us – each night a different man.[1] One evening the maid who is watching me decides we will walk down toward the river to observe the scene. We see many Germans in uniform. Strolling toward us

---

1   Later I learn that Father was a target of the Gestapo because he was both Jewish and a friend and lawyer to the Masaryk family. Since the Gestapo usually made arrests in the middle of the night or just before dawn, my father and his friends who were also in danger exchanged sleeping quarters each night. That way, if the Germans came to arrest one of them in his house, the man would not be home. His family would say that the stranger was a relative, visiting from the country.

comes a group of officers in black. As they advance, a street lamp lights up a silver skull mounted on one of the officers' caps. Terrified, I scream when I see it. The maid rushes me back home.

Upsetting Changes

When we return home, I discover that our upstairs rooms have been closed down. Bewildered, I run up the stairs and wander through the shuttered rooms. Where are my toys, my books? Everything seems in disarray. I am made to sleep in the big music room outside the door to my parents' bedroom. It is a scary night.

When I wake up in the morning, most of the paintings on the first floor of our home have been removed. What does this mean? I run into the big hall outside the music room. There are huge trunks, propped open and half-full of dishes and artwork, with newspapers crumpled between. Mother is filling other trunks with clothing. People keep bringing in more things to be packed. I see the maid with a pile of my clothing in her arms. There is my favorite light blue sweater with red heart-shaped buttons.

Our furniture is turned around, all out of place. Several pieces have stickers with numbers on them. Our paintings are on the floor in the hall, turned toward the wall, with the same stickers and numbers on them. Father's secretary is busy writing numbers on a sheet of paper, making notes next to them. Some of my favorite paintings have disappeared.[2] No one has told me that we are leaving. After a while, I don't need to be told.

Are We Leaving?

I decide to approach Mother. I want my knowledge to be confirmed in spoken words.

"We're leaving, aren't we?" I ask.

Mother kneels down, wrapping her arms around me. "Yes, we are. Things aren't safe here for us any longer, and we are going to America. But Aničko, you must keep this a secret or you'll put us all in danger." Seeing my frightened expression, she adds, "There will be a big World's Fair going on in New York, and we are going to see it. Then we'll come back home."

"I don't believe you!" I shout. "We are not coming back!"

I tear myself away, rushing out of the house and into the street. Turning left, I run on the cobbled sidewalk to the nearby Strahov Monastery.[3] Its beautiful fruit orchard is just

---

2 Later I learn that Father has used several of the paintings to ease the way for the permits and documents we needed to leave the country. Among them was *Portrait of a Gentleman* by Pierre Mignard, referred to earlier.

3 The Strahov (pronounced *stra*-hoff) is a monastery with a beautiful orchard and garden attached to it. The crowning jewel of Strahov is its library, which is decorated with extraordinary frescoes. It is not far from Prague Castle and the St. Vitus Cathedral.

When we lived in Prague, the ruling abbot of the monastery, *Opat Zavoral* (Abbot Zavoral), was a friend of my parents, who held him in the highest esteem. We were told that he was murdered by the Nazis during the German Occupation because he sheltered "enemies of the state."

beginning to bloom in the whites and rosy pinks of early spring. This is my friends' and my favorite place to play. I look for some of them, and sure enough, I see Jana, Ruzenka, and my best friend, Marie, sitting on a bench. I wave and join them.

Marie is dressed just like me, in a sweater and pleated skirt. We are the same height, both of us with light brown braids. But while my eyes are green like Mother's, hers are bright blue. If I had a sister, she would be like Marie.

My friends and I have invented a new game. One of us describes an imagined journey's destination – a city or a country – without naming it. The others guess the name. When my turn comes, I say, "I am going to a country where the houses reach up to the sky and people shoot each other in the street."

"America!" the three of them shout in unison. Marie notices my confused expression and guesses the truth.

"Aničko," she says, "You really *are* going to America, aren't you?" I flush with guilt, because I have betrayed the secret and endangered my family. I run away crying – and never see my friends again.

Goodbyes

The next day, the trunks in the hall are closed. Father returns home, saying we must leave quickly. For the last time, Father, Mother, my brothers, and I walk down the dark staircase that leads to the courtyard. I carry Suzanka, the doll Mother had brought me when she returned from a long concert tour. And I am wearing my new blue coat. Obeying a sudden impulse, I press my hand to the wall of the house and whisper goodbye.

Several people stand in the courtyard waiting to say goodbye – neighbors and people who worked for my parents. Embraces, whispers, tears. Father frowns with anxiety; Mother is pale and silent. I cling to Miss Cook, whose sweet-smelling kitchen has so often been my refuge.

Standing in the group is the nurse who took care of me whenever I was sick. She had taught me my prayers and helped me prepare for my First Communion. I see her take Mother's handbag from her, open it, and stuff two holy pictures inside – one of the Sacred Heart, the other of St. Christopher, patron saint of travelers.

"They will protect you," she tells Mother. Mother smiles, hugs her, and says nothing. Then it is time. Father takes my hand, Mother turns back for one last look at the house. The five of us walk out into the street where our car and driver are waiting. We drive silently down the hill toward the city's center.

Grandmother

Our first stop is the home of my grandmother, an apartment near the river. In spite of Father's pleading, she will not come with us. So we must go to say goodbye. We park and climb the stairs, none of us saying a word. I pinch myself hard so I won't cry. She opens her door and we walk into the familiar apartment that is filled with mementos and pictures of us, our aunts, uncles, cousins, and our dead grandfather.

There are also pictures of her in-laws, our great-grandparents, who spent their lives among the few Jews in Kácov.

Now my brothers and I wait in Grandmother's living room as she and my parents talk.

They stand close together: Father, tall and formal in a dark three-piece suit, with his tie and the gold glint of his watch chain adding the only bit of color; Mother, slight and beautiful in a violet outfit with fur around her throat; and Grandmother, in her customary dark dress that reaches to the floor. I stand frozen, watching them.

Then Grandmother moves toward us, the children. She speaks with my brothers first. I can't hear what she says to them, but her expression is so serious and at the same time so loving. Karel, the oldest of us, embraces her with tears in his eyes. Pavel buries his face in her shoulder.

At last she comes to me. She puts her arms around me, holds me close, and this time I can't stop the tears. I smell her familiar musky cologne. She murmurs some words that I can't understand and kisses me. As we make our way down the stairs, I turn back and see her watching from her landing. I hear her long sigh as we walk out to the street.

CHAPTER 8

THE JOURNEY BEGINS

There is no time for sadness. We have a train to catch. Father hurries us back into the car, and our chauffeur turns toward the train station.

Father's plan is to travel north through Germany to Holland, then by ship to London, where his brother Benno and several friends have gone before us. From there, another sea voyage, this time to New York where "Uncle" Sidney Dietsch, Mother's singing coach and my parents' close friend, will meet us.

Uncle Sidney has agreed to be our American sponsor, and has sent Mother enthusiastic letters about her future in New York, describing the highly paid teaching position that is awaiting her at a distinguished music academy. The letters are a fabrication, designed for my parents to use in their effort to obtain American visas. The trick works, and authorities at the American consulate in Prague are persuaded that a good job is waiting for one of my parents, and thus we will not be a burden in the United States. The visas have been granted.

Once at Masaryk Station, we find our train, board it, and settle into our compartment. I watch through the window as the platform empties, whistles blow, and the train pulls slowly out of the station. As it speeds up, it lurches and rumbles through the Czech countryside, stopping from time to time to let passengers get off and new ones board. Sometimes it stops for what seems to be no reason at all.

A light rain moistens the window as the train moves toward the German border. My parents sit side by side, talking quietly. Karel and Pavel play chess on a portable set whose round, pegged pieces fit into holes in the board. I am frightened, though I don't really know why. Is it my parents' solemn expressions? Is it my memory of our trip to Dresden or of the skull on the German officer's cap in Prague? Perhaps it is the unaccustomed way everything is happening around me. For comfort, I whisper a story to my doll, Suzanka, stroking her hair.

At lunch time, instead of moving to the dining car as we usually do, we eat sandwiches that Miss Cook has packed for us. As we eat, we watch the procession of passengers making their way along the aisle outside our compartment. Most of them are German soldiers. A group stops and stares at us. One soldier points his finger at my brothers and says something that makes them all laugh. Then they move on.

Confrontation

Suddenly, the door of our compartment bursts open. An officer enters and stands over Father. *"Papieren, bitte."* ("Your papers, please.") Father hands him our passports and other documents. The man looks through them carefully, then reaches out his hand for Mother's handbag. He takes out her wallet, opens it, pulls out many bills, then holds them up with an expression of accusation and victory.

Mother has forgotten to empty her wallet before leaving Prague, breaking the strict limitations on the amount of money one could take out of the country. This offense is more than enough to send us back.

A terrible scene follows. The officer shouts a command, ordering us off the train at the next stop. *"Ihr sind juden!"* ("You are Jews!") he screams. Father resists, forcefully, passionately. A contest of wills follows, in German, a language I barely understand. My heart pounding, I hold Suzanka tightly and make myself as small as I can.

Finally, the Gestapo man stops shouting, but continues to rummage through Mother's handbag. He pulls out the two holy pictures and looks intently at Mother. "Are you Catholic?" he asks her.

"Yes," she answers. After a pause, he pockets the money, stuffs the pictures back into her handbag, throws it at Mother's feet, and walks swiftly out of the compartment. We are saved.

CHAPTER 9

DRAGONS AND PRINCES

None of us speak as the train chugs on. The rain lets up, so we can follow changes in the landscape more clearly. Countryside, small villages, no hills now. It begins to get dark outside. "We are almost in Holland," Father says, and I hear relief in his voice.

But then the train lurches to an abrupt stop. A voice crackles over the loudspeaker: *"Alle raus,"* ("Everyone out"). We snatch up our coats and small baggage and step off the train onto the crowded platform.

As we watch our train empty and leave, we are directed into the crowded train station. Mother sighs quietly, "What now? What next?" A station officer makes a loud announcement in German. Leaning down, Father explains that the Dutch will not allow anyone to enter Holland without proof that the person does not intend to stay in the country. This proof must include not only visas, but also train or steamship tickets to other countries. Holland is already overflowing with refugees and no more will be allowed to remain there.

People surround the officer to question, plead, argue. Policemen arrive to keep order. I hear a jumble of languages, feel people pushing in all directions. Some stand in long lines, waiting to show whatever documents they have. Father tells us that a clerk from a Dutch shipping line is selling passage out of Holland at exorbitant prices. People who have neither the required documents nor the money to buy their way out of Holland weep openly.

Anxious Calls for Help

We, too, are in trouble. Father has our American visas with him, but other papers, including ship's passage to New York, are waiting for us in London. And he is almost out of money. But Father is nothing if not resourceful. He finds a public telephone, takes out his address book, and begins calling everyone he knows in Amsterdam – friends, business associates, even distant acquaintances – to ask for help. Mother leads me to a bench, instructs me to sit there and pray, and leaves me to join Father. I don't know where my brothers are.

By now it is very dark outside, and the noise and panic around me are frightening. Many children are crying. I pull my knitted cap way down over my forehead. I don't pray but sit quietly, holding Suzanka and watching the scene before me. More trains arrive, steam and smoke swirling around them, unload their passengers, and leave. More announcements, shouts, arguments. The crowd in the train station begins bursting out onto the street; more police arrive.

People push along in front of me. Where are they going?

I see women with babies. I see older children like me. The boys are dressed like my brothers, some in knickers, some in long pants, sweaters, and caps, lugging knapsacks, dragging suitcases. The girls carry dolls or stuffed animals. Some of them have braids like mine. A woman screams. I am so tired; I huddle on my bench, wanting to disappear. As things grow more and more scary, I close my eyes and imagine that I am playing with my friends in the Strahov orchard.

After what seems like hours, my parents and brothers appear before me with a stranger. He is Albert Andriesse, a businessman Father barely knows. He has responded to Father's plea for help by driving miles across Holland to the Dutch-German border, bringing all that the authorities require. He smiles at me and leads us out of the station to his car, in which he will drive us to his home in Amsterdam.

As we all settle into the car, I stare at the back of our new friend, who slides into the driver's seat. "He is a prince," I think drowsily, "from one of my fairy tales. He has rescued us from the dragon, from its poisonous teeth and claws. He is carrying us to safety in his castle, on his white steed."

CHAPTER 10

AMSTERDAM TO NEW YORK

Though he barely knows us, Mr. Andriesse invites us to stay at his home in Amsterdam for a few days of respite and sightseeing. My parents gratefully agree.

Mother wants us to see Rembrandt's *The Night Watch*, so we accompany her to the Rijksmuseum. She loves this famous painting of a 17th century militia and talks about it for a long time as my brothers and I listen. She points out the unusual placement of figures, the play of light and shadow, and how the captain seems to reach out to the viewer with his hand. My brothers are interested, but my mind is elsewhere. Mrs. Andriesse notices this, and as soon as Mother ends her talk, Mrs. Andriesse says, "Now we'll show you something else."

A Sea of Tulips

She takes my hand, and the two of us lead the group out of the museum. We drive to the outskirts of the city. As we turn a corner I see, suddenly, huge expanses of color: red, yellow, orange, white, and every shade between. They are magical fields. No, they are fields of flowers; they are fields of tulips. The expanses of color seem endless. A slight breeze picks up and the flowers move, all together, as if in a stately dance. I stare and stare. In this time of our reprieve, I am sure I have never seen flowers so beautiful, so joyful. When we finally leave Amsterdam and say goodbye to our friends and rescuers, Mother takes memories of the Rembrandt with her. I take the tulips.

London Chill

We cross the North Sea, and soon we are in London where all of us shiver with the sudden cold. My parents and Father's brother, my Uncle Benno, have an emotional reunion and lengthy conversations late into the night. We visit some friends of my parents in a very elegant hotel called Claridge's, but all I can think about is how painfully cold London is. In the small boarding house where we stay, a coin in the radiator meter buys only one hour of heat. I beg mother for a coin every so often; sometimes I am successful.

Crossing the Ocean

After about a week's stay in London, our ship, the S.S.Washington, is ready to be boarded by its passengers. Uncle Benno will not be traveling with us. He is remaining in London to wait for his son, my cousin Ivan, to travel there from Prague. Ivan is scheduled to be aboard one of the

Kindertransports organized by Nicholas Winton, a young London stockbroker, to rescue Czech Jewish children from German capture and bring them to England.[1] Because both of Ivan's parents are Jewish, he is in great danger as things worsen in Prague. After his safe arrival, we hope to meet Ivan and his father later, in New York, if they can get visas. So we say goodbye to Uncle Benno, and set sail for New York.

After two days at sea, Mother becomes very seasick and takes to her bed in the stateroom my parents and I share. Father stays with her, putting cold compresses on her forehead. Again, I am left on my own. But this time I love the freedom.

I explore the labyrinth of passages on our deck, climb up and down to the other decks, peer into open doors, guess what the lives of the people I see there are like. I run into my brothers and follow them for a while, but they are less than delighted by my dogging their steps, so I take off again on my own.

Back on our deck, I peek into the ballroom and the dining room, where the maitre d' asks me about my parents. When I tell him that Mother is sick, he takes me to our table, holds out a chair for me as he did for my mother, and sees that I am given a royal meal by myself. The most remarkable part of the meal is the dessert: a bowl of banana circles sprinkled

---

1   In 1939, Sir Nicholas Winton quietly arranged for 669 children to be transported by train from Nazi-occupied Czechoslovakia and relocated safely in the United Kingdom. On September 1, the final train was canceled when Hitler invaded Poland, leaving 250 children stranded on the platform and later transported to concentration camps where they presumably perished.

with sugar and cream. We had no bananas in Prague, and I love it. When the bowl is almost empty, I look up and see two waiters watching and smiling at me. I smile back at them as I finish the very last bit of the heavenly treat.

After dinner, I see my first American movie, *The Hound of the Baskervilles*. I understand none of the English dialogue, and I am scared by the frightening background music and the huge, menacing dog – but I feel grown up to be watching a foreign film.

New York At Last

After several days – the New York Harbor. We stand together at the railing and watch as the harbor comes closer and closer. Mother lifts me up high to help me see the Statue of Liberty as clearly as possible. She says, with a kind of fierceness, "Don't ever forget this."

CHAPTER 11

STARTING A NEW LIFE

We land at Ellis Island, and we wait. Father tells us that we're lucky that the procedures are less demanding than in the past, but they still seem to take forever. Lines of lines, up stairs, down corridors, through the Great Hall.

First line: Father presents the passports and visas that have gotten us this far. Second line: my parents must prove that a sponsor is vouching for us. Mother produces Uncle Sidney's letters describing the non-existent teaching positions that are waiting for her. Approved. Now a line in which we must prove our health. Doctors take our temperatures, examine our mouths and eyes, listen to our hearts. At each station I hold my breath, wondering what can go wrong. Finally, we are all given the go-ahead. As we follow the others about to step onto American soil, I see a large open door, and beyond, a crowd of welcomers. I feel a rush of relief when I spot the top of Uncle Sidney's head. He is tall and towers over the others in the welcoming party. When we finally reach him, he greets us all, gives me a big hug, and leads us to his waiting car.

Exploring New York

Uncle Sidney drives us to the furnished apartment he has rented for us at the Franconia Hotel on West 72nd Street. I like it, but Father says it is far too expensive for us and that we will have to move. The next day Uncle Sidney drives us all around New York. That evening he treats us to the Radio City Music Hall, and I see my second American movie. Of course I understand nothing, but I love the high-stepping dancers who entertain during the intermission.

The next several days are filled with more exploration. Central Park is huge, expansive. I don't think it is as beautiful

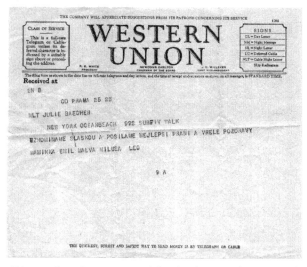

Telegram from Prague, received shortly after arrival in New York

"*We think of you with love and send the best wishes.*
Mother (Grandmother Baecher), *Emil* (Father's uncle), *Malva*
(Father's sister), *Leo and Miluska* (Father's brother and wife)"

as my Strahov Garden, but there is a wonderful playground. We walk up Fifth Avenue and peer into the elegant storefront windows. We explore the Metropolitan Museum of Art. Mother and Father have both been there before, when Mother came for a tour in the United States in the early 1930s. They talk to us about many of the paintings.

We walk east and south, and finally end up on York Avenue, where the languages I hear gradually change from English to German and, eventually, to Czech. Guidebook in hand, Father explains that New York is full of different ethnic neighborhoods. We pass a church named the Jan Hus Church.

We spot a Czech bakery, a Czech butcher shop that sells the sausages we love, and three Czech restaurants. We stop for lunch in one of them – baked duck and dumplings, just as if we were still in Prague.

As the explorations continue, I pay special attention to all that is different from our life in Prague: wide boulevards, huge crowds, unbelievably tall buildings, people with dark skins, the sounds of many languages I have never heard before, subways, escalators, supermarkets, cafeterias, Chinese food, Woolworth's five-and-ten-cent stores, chewing gum, hamburgers on buns, ice cream sodas. And more.

For a special outing, Uncle Sidney takes my brothers and me to the Barnum and Bailey Circus. I have been to the little fairs that came to Kácov some summers, but this is something new. Elephants, acrobats on horseback, trapeze artists, tightrope walkers, trained tigers, jugglers, and clowns. It's all so extraordinary. At one point, a small car appears in the central ring. Clowns in silly costumes keep tumbling out, turning somersaults, standing on each others' heads, forming human pyramids. Those clowns stay with me longer than I expect.

Night Fears

For a long time after our arrival, I am afraid to fall asleep unless someone is in the room with me. Usually Father sits patiently until I nod off. When he can't, one of my brothers takes his place. I have a recurring nightmare that prowls through my dreams. Pursued by some unseen terror, I am running to get into a little car like the one I saw in the circus. A driver sits at the wheel. We try to leave but we can't because there is someone else running to escape along with me, and then someone else, and someone else again. We never take off, and just as the pursuer is ready to pounce, I wake up in a cold sweat. Perhaps my brothers also have fears, but I never hear about them. They are older and keep to themselves.

Moving West

The year marches on, and we move further west on 72nd Street. Our new home is in a shabby three-story building. The landlady, Mrs. Kostomiris, is a heavy, middle-aged woman with frizzy black and gray hair. She always wears a flowered housedress and has sharp, dark eyes and a mouth that rarely smiles. She knocks on our door at odd hours and comes in to "inspect." What is she looking for?

There are six apartments in the three-flat. Mother thinks that the other tenants are friends or relatives of Mrs.

Kostomiris, and we are the only "outsiders." Perhaps that's why she is so uncomfortable with us. Whatever the reason, she seems to spend most of her day on a folding chair in front of the house, keeping a sharp lookout on strangers she doesn't recognize – and on us. I seem to be a special subject of interest. "Where are you off to now, Missy?" she calls out to me every time I leave the building. I answer politely, as I have been taught to do, in my few English words.

For all her fussing, the building is not well kept. There are cobwebs in the corners of the dimly lit stairwell and cockroaches in our kitchen, no matter what we do to keep things clean. I am afraid of the cockroaches, and I am afraid of Mrs. Kostomiris.

Mother's Struggles

Mother speaks little English, and she does not seek out the job Uncle Sidney had imagined for her. She becomes ill and is bedridden with a severe case of rheumatoid arthritis. I am sure that at least part of her illness is the pain of leaving Prague. Having grown up without a father, then losing her strong mother at an early age, she feels especially connected to the beautiful city of her birth, its history, its sheltering hills and gardens. Perhaps losing the city, and even its language, is more than she can bear.

Mother doesn't make much of an effort to improve her English. As a singer, she knows not only Czech and German, but also Italian, beautiful French, some Russian, as well as bits and pieces of other languages. But her English remains garbled.

Protector and Guardian

With Mother's protracted illness, Father is the caregiver of all of us. He nurses Mother, who at first is barely able to get out of bed. He waits on her with meals and baths, and supervises her medications. And he manages the home.

And there are his efforts at cooking. I had never seen him even step into our kitchen in Prague. Now he is taking up meal preparation with gusto. My brothers and I swallow tasteless food and crunch undercooked rice, and tell him how delicious it all is. And Father braids my pigtails – not very well – every morning before I leave for school.

While he is caring for us, Father also throws his prodigious energy into finding new ways of making a living. At the age of fifty-plus, he finds this difficult. Law is closed to him, since he lacks the language as well as education in the basics of American law. So he turns to business. He spends his days seeking out contacts and opportunities, spending hours meeting new acquaintances, talking on the telephone night after night, discussing possible prospects.

Many of Father's meetings take place in The Éclair, a café on West 72nd Street opposite the Franconia apartment hotel in which we lived when we first arrived in New York. From time to time he takes me with him for special treats. They serve coffee or hot chocolate with whipped cream, together with the most wonderful European-style pastries: Malakoff and Dobosh tortes, and of course, éclairs. The walls are covered with central European newspapers – German, Czech, Slovak, Hungarian – and those are the languages I hear spoken by most of the customers. English is the only language I hardly ever hear in the café. I love the place.

Father doesn't like The Éclair as much as I do, however. He says it is good for meeting fellow European refugees, but he is scornful of the criticism of American culture one can hear from people at other tables. "How foolish they are," he tells me. "Being here is a new opportunity, a new beginning for all of us. We are so lucky."

Passionately eager to understand America and become part of it, Father decides he must learn proper English and lose his accent. He hires Miss Reed, a retired high school English teacher, to tutor him. They discuss Shakespeare, and Father memorizes soliloquies from *Hamlet* to practice his English. At night, he marches through our apartment, reciting *"To be or not to be, that is the question..."* in his thick Central European accent. I admire his determination, though I also giggle a bit to myself. Of course his English never becomes great, and he never loses his accent as he had hoped. But he never gives up trying.

We live sparingly. For celebrations, there are occasional meals at the Horn and Hardart Automat or at a nearby Chinese restaurant, The Good Earth, both on West 72nd Street. My favorite restaurant is a Greek diner. We sit on stools and eat at a bright green Formica-covered bar that surrounds the proprietor, who dishes out the food. Like Miss Cook, he thinks I am much too skinny, so he gives me extra big portions.

CHAPTER 12

FINDING OUR WAY

When we emigrated to America, my parents left behind them dinners at elegant restaurants; trips to Venice, Barcelona, and Paris; and clothes designed by fine couturiers. But there is one luxury they can not give up – concerts.

The Necessary Luxury

Many of Europe's finest musicians have fled Hitler's Europe just as we did, and New York is full of events featuring these artists. One is a series of concerts at Town Hall, sponsored by the New Friends of Music. These are concerts of chamber music as well as solo recitals by singers and instrumentalists.

My parents subscribe to these weekly events. They always take me with them, or I go with just Father when Mother is too ill. I attend at least two, perhaps three "farewell concerts" by Lotte Lehmann, a famous lieder singer. Each time she is honored with endless standing ovations. There is always a cacophony of languages during intermissions; the concerts seem to be a magnet for refugees from all of Europe. I'm not particularly grateful to my parents for taking me with them. As a ten-year-old girl, my musical interest is developing in another direction.

Schooling

It is fall, and my brothers enroll in George Washington High School in uptown Manhattan. They have been well prepared by the Czech high school, called a gymnasium, which they had attended in Prague. Since they had studied English, they speak the language better than anyone else in our family. Also, there are many refugee teenagers at the school. So Karel and Pavel have quickly become Charlie and Paul, buddying up with new friends.

Pavel and Karel become Paul and Charlie

My brothers do well in school. I am not so lucky. There are few immigrant families in our neighborhood, and the public elementary school I am enrolled in has little experience with children like me. So even though I had almost completed the fifth grade in Prague, I am "put back" into fourth grade on the assumption that having easy material to study will help me focus on the language. I tower over the other children, and I am ashamed. "They think I'm stupid," I complain to Mother.

There is another immigrant in my class – a boy who speaks German. I speak a little German, and so I think he will be my bridge to the new American world. But he thinks it will be fun to give me misinformation. When I ask him to tell me what the social studies homework is, he says that I need to memorize a certain page in the book and be prepared to recite it in class the next day. I, of course, cannot do this, because I cannot even read the page. I go home and weep over my inability to even read English, much less to memorize long passages.

One day an artist comes to my school. She is looking for a "typical American child" to use as a model for some sketches she is preparing for a new reader. After looking over our class, she chooses me. A message is brought to my teacher that I am to come down to the principal's office. I go down, feeling bitter; I assume I am about to be put back into third grade because my English is so poor. When I speak to the principal and the artist in my broken English, they look astonished. Without explanation, the principal sends me back to my class, where the children stare at me, thinking I had been in trouble of some kind.

Later that week my teacher tells my parents, with something of an embarrassed apology, that I was not used as the model because I wasn't "American." My parents tell me that I am *their* best American and the story becomes something of a family joke. "Meet my American daughter," Father says to a friend, his arm around me. "Here comes my American sister," says Charlie, and we laugh at the foolishness of it all.

More Education

Every afternoon when I come home from school, I seek out Mother, who is eagerly waiting for me. "What did you learn today?" she asks.

I answer as best I can. One day I tell her, "Today I learned how they do long division here. It's simple. I got my first 'A' ever."

"Wonderful!" she says. But arithmetic isn't my problem. It is the language.

Another day: "Today I learned that the letter "o" followed by the letter "u" is pronounced in four different ways in English. Listen to this: "through – loud – rough – bought."

"Did the teacher show you this?" Mother asks.

"No, I figured it out myself, after I flunked the spelling test."

And on another day: "Today I learned hopscotch. I wasn't any good."

"Did the teacher help you?"

"Oh mother," I say, "Teachers don't teach you hopscotch. This was during recess. The other girls teach you hopscotch."

Mother bites her lip, perhaps to avoid asking, "What is recess?"

And another day, a year or so later: "Today I learned that they bought and sold people in this country, years ago. Here, in America! They called them slaves. They were brought over on ships from Africa."

"What did the teacher say about this?" Mother asks.

"She said we'd have a date quiz next Wednesday."

"Did she say anything else?"

"Nothing."

"*Nothing?*"

"No, nothing." I learn a lot from that teacher's nothing.

New York Christmas

At first my brothers are the family's only wage earners. They find jobs delivering groceries in the neighborhood after school. All fall and early winter, they save their money. They buy a wind-up record player and some records as a surprise Christmas present for our parents.

On that first Christmas Eve in America, my brothers make the three of us – Father, Mother and me – wait in darkness outside the living room door, in a re-enactment of our Prague Christmases. Suddenly – lights, and the door opens on a small Christmas tree and the sounds of Dvořák's "Slavonic Dance No. 3." I watch Mother embrace each of her sons, with tears in her eyes.

Later that Christmas Eve, a messenger knocks on the door. Uncle Sidney has sent a large shopping bag full of beautifully wrapped presents for me and my brothers. For me, there are games, a purse, jewelry perfect for a young girl, a pretty blouse, books. Uncle Sidney must have guessed that we would compare this Christmas with the ones that had come before. Whatever he thinks, he has made this American Christmas special. I love my American uncle.

A Surprising Request

One evening the doorbell rings, and there stands my brother Paul's employer, the grocer for whom Paul makes deliveries. He is dressed in a dark suit and looks very solemn. He asks to speak to Father.

As the two men sit together, he tells Father he wants to adopt Paul. "What can you do for him here?" he asks. "If he becomes my son, he'll inherit the store, the business, he'll have a good life."

Father thanks him for the honor, gently rejects the request, and turns the conversation to the war in Europe, which is in a perilous state.

Paul and Pavel, father and son

France has capitulated. The London Blitz is escalating. Father's anxiety is at a peak. But his guest's thoughts are elsewhere. He leaves disappointed.

Unexpected Arrival

After many months, a wonderful surprise. The furniture, paintings, and huge trunks that were packed before we left Prague have arrived. It is hard for anyone to understand how, in the middle of the European war, these things haven't been destroyed, haven't been stolen, or didn't drown, but here they are.

The Baecher family, NYC, 1940

Father sells some art objects, and we move again, this time into a larger, unfurnished apartment further west, overlooking the Hudson River. I am thrilled to say goodbye to Mrs. Kostomiris.

Our new home is furnished mostly with the pieces that have come from Prague. They help me to feel more comfortable, but at the same time they remind me of the home I have lost and I feel a little sad. "Yes," I think to myself, "this corner cupboard stood in our dining room. This desk was in my parents' bedroom."

My parents have hired a woman named Mary Goetz to help with the housekeeping. Mary speaks the language of Czechs who have immigrated long before us, a kind of Czech peppered with English words that have been given Czech endings. She cooks the soup with liver dumplings and the *palačinky* – delicate, thin crepes rolled up with preserves or a sweet cheese mixture and sprinkled with confectioner's sugar – that we knew from Prague. I love her.

Julia and Anna

CHAPTER 13

HOMESICK

Our new city has so many interesting things to see: giant buildings and ships, broad boulevards with elegant shops, parades more colorful and surprising than any I have seen in Prague. Our new surroundings often astonish me, but I cannot let go of memories of our old life. I think of Prague often.

New York's pavements are so sturdy and gray. I miss the pink, light blue, and gray cobblestones of Prague streets, where I often played my private games of counting their shapes and colors. I miss the many-colored stucco houses in our quarter. I miss Miss Cook's tender, thin noodles baked with farmer's cheese and raspberry sauce, though Mary's version is also good. I miss the delicious drinks Miss Cook made to "fatten me up." I miss her stories of life in her home village.

I miss our house, my room with its bright windows, my toys and books, which had to be left behind. I miss Grandmother and our games. I miss Marie and playing with my friends in the Strahov garden. I miss our country place in Kácov, the tortoise, the garden with its smells of roses, the scary bee houses. I miss swimming in the sweet waters of the Sazava River with Father. Now that his mind is on more serious things, he no longer has time or inclination for swims. I miss Prague.

Bullied

Nothing seems to help my homesickness. And I am unhappy at school. The teachers do not offer to help me with the new sounds and meanings of English. The only "help" they have given is to put me into fourth grade, and that has its own problems. I am often called up to my teacher's desk to explain something incomprehensible that I have written. I am sure that she is kind and wants to help me, but I am still ashamed.

It all makes me think of frightening stories about the way some children are taught to swim here in America. Instead of being taught gently as I was by Father, they are thrown into a pool, into water over their heads. The shock of this must be terrible. Am I being taught English the same way – by being thrown into a pool full of English words and idioms, tumbling and bubbling all together? Sink or swim? I wonder.

My relations with the other children in school make things even worse. They just don't know what to make of me; they think I am an odd duck. I wonder if maybe they are right. They find my clothing funny and my speech laughable. Some girls follow me as I walk home from school, mimicking my odd pronunciation of words and phrases that they had heard me struggle with in class that day. They speak loudly enough to make sure I hear them.

As my English improves and they hear the teacher praise me, they keep up their mockery, shouting "teacher's pet" after me. I can't win, but at this point, I don't care. I certainly don't want to complain to my parents. They have enough to worry about. So I keep my troubles to myself.

American Birthday

We have been in the United States nearly a year, and my eleventh birthday is approaching. Mother tells me to invite three girls from my class to come for a celebration. I pick carefully, avoiding the bullies. The girls I invite come, and they bring presents. Mother serves hot chocolate with whipped cream and éclairs, but no cake with writing on it, no candles for me to blow out. The girls sing a song that I have never heard before. Its words include "happy birthday" and my American name, "Anna." That is nice. I thank them for the presents, and I think they liked the éclairs, but they seem puzzled as they leave. This was a different kind of birthday party, not what they had expected.

I enjoy my party, but I miss my Prague birthday celebrations – a wonderful cake baked by Grandmother, a flag outside my door in the morning, and Mother's puppet show, with Princess Anička in the starring role.

CHAPTER 14

TRYING TO BECOME AN AMERICAN GIRL

I have survived a year of American school, and things are getting better. I still miss my old life, but my English is improving, and now I can make sense of the classroom reading assignments. But I am puzzled by the differences between me and the other girls in school.

I begin to study my classmates carefully. Why do they laugh at things that are different from the things that make me laugh? Why are they comfortable in the very situations that confuse me and make me uneasy? What does it take to be an American girl? What does she talk about? What does she wear? What does she like? I want to fit in, to become more like these girls. I notice that there is one thing that American girls really like – pop tunes. And I don't know any.

The Wrong Music

My home is full of music. But it is the wrong kind of music. Mother is still too ill to take part in musical activities, but whenever he has time, Father plays Chopin mazurkas and intermezzi on the piano. Charlie and Paul play Schubert études and practice their cello and piano scales and exercises. I am expected to follow suit, but I just don't take to it. Instead, I stage a small rebellion and teach myself to sing off key. Charlie catches on to my ruse, but I persist.

I buy myself a small radio, and Saturday night becomes the most exciting time of my week. I crawl into bed, pull the blanket up over the radio and my head, and listen to *The Lucky Strike Hit Parade*. It is great fun, but I also take it very seriously. Slowly I learn the songs of the day: "Sentimental Journey," "Night and Day," "The Chattanooga Choochoo," and "White Christmas," sung by Bing Crosby. What could be better?

I know that I am onto a good thing, and decide to expand my horizons. What about soap operas? I listen to them whenever I am home during the day. I hear *Ma Perkins*, *Backstage Wife*, and *Portia Faces Life*. And there are the evening dramas, like *The Lone Ranger*.

As my self-education in becoming an American girl continues, so does my parents' social life. In spite of Mother's illness, they continue to entertain, with the help of our wonderful Mary Goetz. Their guests are mostly European émigré musicians. Their favorite is Fritz Busch, the German conductor who, like Toscanini, refused to live under the totalitarian boot. He was not Jewish, so he could have stayed safely where he was well known and loved. Before he left Europe, he conducted Europe's greatest orchestras, and he often used my mother as his soprano soloist. Now he was starting with new venues and new audiences. But no one was telling him what music his orchestra may or may not play, and that made all the difference.

On one particular evening, Busch and his wife Grete were at our place for dinner while I tuned up my radio. There was my program. There was the introductory music. Suddenly, the door bursts open. It is Fritz Busch.

"Ah, Anushka, Toscanini?" He assumes I am listening to a broadcast of the *William Tell Overture*, conducted by Toscanini. No, Fritz. It isn't Toscanini. It isn't "William Tell." It is *The Lone Ranger*, using the *William Tell Overture* for its opening theme. Fritz realizes his mistake and quickly closes the door, but not before he hears the immortal opening phrase "Heigh-ho, Silver! The Lone Ranger rides again."

How to Dress

I am learning about the right kind of American music, but dressing is quite another challenge. One of the big trunks that arrived so unexpectedly from Europe contains a coat for me – a floor-length peasant sheepskin coat, with flowers and birds embroidered beautifully on the front. I am the only girl in New York with such a coat, and I hate it.[1] I long for a coat like the ones my classmates wear – wool, three-quarter-length, and of one color. Finally Mother relents and takes me shopping downtown.

Standing next to Mother in the crowded bus going home,

---

1   Years later, I saw such coats advertised for high prices in *The New Yorker*. But in the early 1940s, when all I wanted to do was fit in with the other girls, it was not the coat for me.

I keep looking down, running my hands over the smooth fabric of my new coat, relishing its redness. Suddenly I hear the woman sitting in front of us in the bus say, "Somebody has a new coat." The three of us – the woman, Mother, and I – smile at each other as if in happy conspiracy.

Citizenship

As soon as they qualify, my parents apply for American citizenship. This is, of course, Father's decision, and Mother follows suit. Father does not want to return to Europe after the war. He assumes that most of his properties would surely have been confiscated and dispersed, and he expects that most of his dearest friends and relatives would be dead or would have emigrated to other parts of the world. He has made new connections and is on to what he sees as the next stage of his life. He is convinced that it is time to move forward. Much like me, he wants to become an American. He also decides that we will change the spelling of our name from Baecher to a more American version, Backer.

Father is the first to meet all the citizenship requirements, and he receives a formal letter telling him to attend a ceremony on a particular date. Since I am under age, I will become a citizen simply by taking part in the swearing-in ceremony with him. I go, proudly, wearing my new red coat.

We arrive at a huge outdoor plaza. There are many people; I spot some Asians, Hispanics, Europeans, smiling, excited, speaking many languages. The featured speaker addresses us briefly. We are told to hold up our right hand

and swear allegiance to the United States. My father and I do so. Afterwards, as Father gets involved in a long discussion with the Frenchman sitting next to him, I sit quietly and think about what has just happened. I am now an American. What does this mean? Am I losing my Czech origins? Or am I now an American with Czech roots? And most importantly, what kind of American do I want to become?

CHAPTER 15

A DIFFERENT KIND OF SUMMER CAMP

Most of the girls in my class go to some sort of summer camp. We had nothing like this in Europe; I spent my vacations in Kácov. So I wonder about these American "camps." Would I want to go to one? Could I? I soon have an answer.

Alice Masaryk, daughter of the founding president of Czechoslovakia and my mother's close friend, came to the United States when we did and made her home near us in New York City. She stays in close touch with Mother, and she takes a special interest in me because she is my godmother.

One of Alice's friends is a retired Shakespearean actress named Katherine Everts. She directs a summer camp for girls and has told Alice that she wants to invite girls who were displaced by the war to come to her camp for the summer of 1940. Alice recommended me, and that is how I am headed to Camp Arden in Vermont, as Katherine's guest.

Father takes me to New York's Grand Central Station to join the other campers, and then he says goodbye. I know no one else in the group, and I am scared. We travel by train to Brattleboro, Vermont, and are then driven in a bus-like truck to the camp nearby.

My First American Friend

When we arrive, I am directed to the cabin where I will be staying. Opening the door, I see a girl roughly my age bouncing on a bed, singing a silly song – typical pre-teen humor – to the tune of Dvořák's "Humoresque." Of course I recognize the tune immediately. Coming from a family that approaches all music – particularly when it is composed by the Czech Antonin Dvořák – with reverence, and having started to rebel against my parents' ponderous seriousness on the subject, I instantly love the song and the singer.

This is Nan, my first long-time American friend.[1] Our beds are next to each other. She introduces me to a number of other songs and games, and she defends me angrily when others make fun of my speech.

I love the camp as much as I love my new friend. Aunt Katherine, as we call the camp director, says that no girl is too young to try to understand Shakespeare, and no music is too difficult to tackle. So I learn lines from *As You like It*, and with the puny voice of which I had been ashamed, I sing three and four-part Bach chorales conducted by Klaus Liepmann,[2]

---

1   Both Nan and I returned to Camp Arden for several summers. We became close friends. When I was a sophomore at Barnard College, she transferred there as a junior, and we became inseparable.

2   Klaus, as we all called him, was an inspiring teacher who helped me overcome some of my feelings of inadequacy with regard to classical music.

a German refugee. Aunt Katherine says that all of us are stars. I lap it up, loving the openness and acceptance she offers.

Another Dvořák Song

When I return from Arden that summer, our parents decide that they would also like a vacation. So we all drive to the Poconos where, friends from Prague tell us, we'll be reminded of the mountains back home. We stay in a lodge. Mother and Father take long walks, my brothers play soccer with a few other boys, and I work on my English by reading a book I brought with me.

After dinner people gather in the lounge where they play cards and other games. There is an upright piano in the corner and some guests find a songbook. Mother is willing to accompany them, so they sing "My Old Kentucky Home" and other American songs. Then someone says, "How about 'Songs My Mother Taught Me?'" He opens the songbook to the right page, and plants it in front of Mother. She plays the introduction and they all begin singing. Suddenly I see that Mother's face is wet with tears.

What is making her weep? I wonder. Is she recalling how she performed this song and others on the concert stage, accompanied by Dvořák's own son-in-law, Josef Suk? Is she remembering the grand piano in the music room of

---

He was an excellent violinist, performing as a soloist in Europe, and later in America. After immigrating to the U.S., he taught at Yale. In 1947, he moved to M.I.T., where he developed an impressive program that joined music to the humanities. He was affectionately called the "Father of Music at M.I.T."

her Prague house, where Suk played while the two of them worked on the interpretation of Dvořák songs? Is it the contrast between that piano and this rickety off-key upright here in the lodge? Or is it simply a wave of profound memories washing over her? How could I know all that she feels. But I, too, have an ache and put my arm around her shoulder as she plays.

Adjustments to the New Life

Year after year I spend my summers at Arden. And each time I return home, I find that things have become better. Mother's health improves, and she finds new ways to channel her talents. Although she doesn't return to singing, she coaches voice students. Mother is eager to make connections with other Czech émigrés and long-time Czech-Americans to promote Czech culture, so she is constantly arranging a variety of public events, primarily concerts. The most important of these is a gala performance of Dvořák's *New World Symphony* by the New York Philharmonic in Carnegie Hall, on which she and Alice Masaryk collaborate. Mother's friend, the Czech conductor Rafael Kubelík, guest-conducts the orchestra.

Father has overcome his early difficulties as well. He has found a partner, and the two of them have started a small insurance company that has become successful. He has not given up his wish to know and understand our new country. Through some happy accident that I cannot explain, he has met a man who is a strong advocate for the rights of minorities and is also interested in immigrants and their adjustment to American life. A member of the board of directors of the NAACP, Alfred Baker Lewis is a distinguished author and speaker. How they met and why Lewis is interested in Father, I don't know. Perhaps Father's background as attorney for the Masaryk family interested him.

Whatever the reason, Mr. Lewis and Father have several conversations, two of them at our house. He questions Father about his work in Europe and tells him about his own work in the NAACP, about racism in this country, about racial segregation and lynchings in the South. I sit in, quietly listening. My understanding is limited, but I know something about injustice and I am fired up. Perhaps becoming an American is about more than just wearing the right coat or knowing the pop tunes of the day.

So, each of us in our own way is becoming part of the American fabric. But the biggest role of all, by my brothers Charles and Paul, is yet to come.

CHAPTER 16

WORLD WAR II

On December 7, 1941, our world changes once again. The Japanese attack Pearl Harbor, and the United States enters World War II. Suddenly we are fighting on two fronts – in Europe and in Asia – and at first the news is disheartening. We lose island after island in the Pacific, London is under constant bombardment, and the only other major country still resisting Hitler's aggression is the Soviet Union.

Father spreads out maps of all the sites on our kitchen table and studies them daily with great anxiety. I peer at the maps with him. The Pacific theatre is beyond me, but I do understand something of the European story.

I ask Father: "How come that Stalin is now a friend of ours? I thought he was a friend of Hitler's." Father explains that Stalin changed sides and that it is to our advantage that someone, besides England, is fighting Hitler on the European continent. But I am still puzzled.

My classmates and I collect cans and roll tinfoil into large balls to bring to school. We save our quarters to buy saving stamps. After they graduate from high school, my brothers are drafted. Charlie is the first to go; he is sent to the Pacific. Some months later Paul is sent to North Africa, and then to join the invasion of Italy. Neither of my brothers is ever involved in direct combat, but they come close. Charlie is decorated for his courage, although we are never told the details.

Wartime Letters

Mother and Father write to each of my brothers daily. They write back regularly, and Paul even writes to me. He has found a close friend who has just graduated from Harvard with a major in English. The two talk a lot about literature, and Paul relates many of their conversations to me in his letters. I am flattered. "Have you read *The Great Gatsby*?" Paul writes, or "I really like the poems of Gerard Manley Hopkins. Also, have a look at some poems by Robert Frost." I love that he wants to talk to me about such things. I am just starting high school, and this is the beginning of my love of poetry.

Eventually both of my brothers come home on leave, Charlie first. I am startled by his appearance. He has matured and looks very handsome.

Not Always Welcome

On Charlie's first day home, he and I go shopping for groceries with Father. We stop at a delicatessen that is a favorite of ours and, it seems, of the whole neighborhood. As usual, there is a large crowd of customers waiting to be served.

When Father's turn comes, he starts to order in his thick Czech accent. The salesman cannot understand him. A woman behind him sneers, "Why don't you go back where you came from?" Charlie turns around to face her, looking so fit and handsome, so American in his army uniform, and says "You can't talk to my father that way." Total silence falls over the place. I am proud.

I have seen other incidents that show we aren't always welcome. One story involves a visit to see my cousin Ivan.

A while ago now, Ivan made it safely from Prague to London on Nicholas Winton's Kindertransport. Once there, he and his father, my Uncle Benno, wanted to come to the United States. Uncle Sidney agreed to be their sponsor as well as ours, so Ivan and Uncle Benno were able to join us in New York.

Uncle Benno, Ivan, Julia, and Pavel

Ivan, who is about my age, has managed to find a summer job at a resort in Michigan. So we all decide to go to visit him. Since Paul is home on leave, he drives us in a rented car.

As we approach Ivan's resort, we see a large sign: "This is a restricted community."

"What does that mean?" I ask.

"It means they don't want Jews," my uncle laughs. "It means that I am not allowed to visit my own son here."

"I thought this happens only in Europe," I say.

"No, my dear, it's a disease you'll find in a lot of places," my father answers.

CHAPTER 17

POSTCARDS FROM PRAGUE

When the war first starts, we have almost no information about life in occupied Europe. Then, some months after the outbreak, Father receives a postcard from our chauffeur back in Prague. He has stayed on as the janitor of our house, which is now occupied by a German general. The postcard tells Father, by pre-arranged code, that a few days after we left, the Gestapo arrived to arrest Father. Fortunately, he had already left.

The news does not surprise either of my parents. They talk about it openly in front of me and I share their relief. Father speaks anxiously about his friends, who were in the same danger as he. But there is no additional news.

Even though they do not receive mail, my parents keep sending telegrams, letters, and cards to family members in Prague to tell them about our arrival in New York and to ask how they are doing. I write as well – to my grandmother. We are hopeful that a card from a girl to her grandmother has a better chance of getting through the censors than one written by an adult. I wait and wait for an answer, but no mail seems to be getting through.

Then one happy day, a card arrives, addressed to me. It is from Grandmother. The card says:

My darling girl: You have no idea how happy you made me with your card. You know how I think of all of you constantly. I am pleased that you like your school. I hope your brothers feel the same way. You surprised me when you said in your card that you are going to meet Nanynka Nohel. I am sure you will like her. Stay healthy and happy, my darling.

— Your devoted Grandmother

I had referred to Nanynka Nohel in my card to Grandmother because my parents asked me to. That was their way of letting her and others in Prague know that the Nohels, who were relatives of ours, had escaped from Europe successfully.

What mattered the most to me was Grandmother's card itself, that she had written and addressed it to me, Aničko. Of course my parents read it many times. The other side of the card was a message to them from Grandmother and Father's youngest brother, my Uncle Leo and his wife, Miluska. The message was one of reassurance about their situation. The three of them were living together now, they said, all in good health and comfort.

Of course, my parents had doubts about that. Uncle Leo and his wife had chosen not to emigrate when we did. Their beloved son, their only child, had died in 1936. My Aunt Miluska refused to leave Prague because she wanted to stay near her son's grave.[1] So they stayed behind.

Mother put the postcard in her desk for safekeeping, first asking me for permission.

Shortly after Grandmother's card, we receive a telegram from Uncle Leo. It contains the following message, in German: "We are well, Mother is with us. Do not worry about us."

Later, a postcard from Leo with the same message.

Finally, one more message in German, a telegram: "This is to inform you that Mother died on June 22nd, 1941." All of us are heartbroken.

Then silence.

---

1   Many people who did not emigrate, even if they had the opportunity (which many did not), had reasons for not leaving that were persuasive to them – thoughts that the German invasion would be short-lived, anxiety about starting a new life in another country at an advanced age, unwillingness to leave loved ones behind, fear of the unknown – as well as curious reasons such as the one that convinced my uncle and aunt that they must stay in Prague.

READING BETWEEN THE LINES

In their correspondence from Europe during the war, my family, as did many Jewish families, worded their letters very carefully. The real intent of messages was often hidden between the written lines.

Sometimes, as between Father and our chauffeur, code words and phrases were arranged ahead of time. A casual mention of a name could be a signal that a relative had escaped safely, as with my reference to Nanynka Nohel in my card to Grandmother. And we often used metaphors. In Uncle Leo's postcard, his reference to keeping house the way my parents did when they were first married told us that they were living very modestly with few means.

The family probably overstated how well they were doing so that my parents wouldn't worry. But there were clues that all was not well. When Grandmother lived in the apartment I knew and write about, her daughter Malva and family were living right across the street. So Grandmother's move to live with Leo was not motivated by the family's fear for her safety. More likely, the pressure had begun for Jews to "double up," particularly those living in an apartment by themselves.

12.X,1939

Moji drazí ! Právě došly Vaše dopisnice ze
dne 15. září na maminku, strýce Emila a Faninku.
Doufám, že jste zatím obdrželi též můj lístek øde-
slaný začátkem září. O nás si nemusíte dělat
skutečně žádné starosti, jsme všichni zdrávi a
žijeme v úplném klidu. Především to platí o mamince
do nového prostředí u nás se dobře vžila. Zatím
jsme asi do konce října ve starém bytě, potom
Praha XII., Záhřebská 37. S Bennou jsme v dosti
pravidelném kontaktu. Doma hospodaříme asi tak,
jako Vy v prvních letech ve Vocelově ulici .
Srdečně Vás všechny pozdravuji Váš

Moje drahý milované děti!
S velkou radostí jsme obdrželi tese lístky.
Jsem šťastné, že jste vsechny zdrávi. Také nám
se daří zdravotně dobře. Zvláště mě je tedy
moc dobře. už jsem si zde úplně zvykla.
Tisíckrát všas zdraví a líbá babička

October 12, 1939

My dear ones ! We just received your letter dated
September 15th, addressed to Mother, Uncle Emil and Fanynka.
I hope that at the same time you received my postcard, mailed in
the beginning of September. Have no worries about us. We are all
well and live in complete comfort. Particularly important is that
Mother is now used to living with us. We will be in our old home
till the end of October. Then we'll move to Zahrebska 37, Prague
12. I am in touch with Benno quite frequently. We keep house the
way you did when you were first married, on Vocelova Street.
Heartfelt greetings to all Your *Leo*

My dear, beloved children!
We received your cards with great joy. I am happy that you are all
in good health. We, too, as well. I, particularly, am in good shape.
I am happily used to living here.
A thousand greetings and kisses, Babička

CHAPTER 18

THE END OF THE WAR

VE Day – May 8, 1945. The end of the war in Europe. We can't stop smiling. Father, ever the realist, says he probably would not recognize Europe as it is today – in shambles, cities bombed out, precious buildings destroyed, homeless people seeking shelter. "That's what modern war does," he says, "but think of the alternative. The Nazi plague is defeated. Let's celebrate, all of us." We have a wonderful dinner and he opens a special bottle of champagne.

Next, the bombing of Hiroshima and Nagasaki, in August. I can hardly comprehend all that atomic war means in this new world. Father says little about it, but he looks solemn. The Japanese surrender and both of my brothers come home. They seem older, more serious. Mother's eyes are shining. Both her sons have returned, safe and sound.

Charlie and Paul have come home just in time to attend my high school graduation. I surprise them with the news: their little sister is valedictorian of her class. I'm not comfortable with all the fuss, but it is true that I studied hard and worked to learn English well enough to deliver my valedictory address practically without an accent.

I have been writing and rewriting my speech for weeks, practicing it in front of the mirror to be ready for the day. I want to say that all of us can be valedictorians, one way or another. I want to make my parents proud. I think of my grandmother. I want to talk about our future, knowing nothing about it. But I think to myself that I am on the right path.

As I stand at the podium, giving my long-rehearsed speech, I see Mother, Father, Charlie, and Paul right in the front row. My parents look proud. Charlie has an ironic look, but when our eyes meet, he gives me a broad smile. When I finish, I get a round of applause, from the adults – parents and teachers – as well as my classmates. That makes me very happy.

But now what? Father has done well in his new business, but he still doesn't have the means to send me away to college. And we don't know much about applying for scholarships. So, I apply to be a day-student at Barnard College, the women's branch of Columbia University in New York.

Barnard College

I thrive at Barnard. Course after course helps me spread my wings: art history, contemporary literature, Russian literature, philosophy. Father is so pleased when I tell him that I have decided to major in European history.

As an upper classman, I am permitted to take graduate courses at Columbia. I jump at the chance to study American history with the well-known historian Henry Steele Commager.

My cousin Ivan, who is studying at the Union Theological Seminary, takes me to hear Reinhold Niebuhr preach at the Riverside Church. W. H. Auden comes to Barnard to teach a course on opera, a special interest of his, but I am too stuck in my old anxieties about opera to enroll in it, which I soon regret.

Post-War Revival, Meeting Jan Masaryk

All around me, returning GIs are entering universities and colleges in increasing numbers. They are finding jobs, buying homes on government loans. There is much hope in the air. The United Nations has been created, and the world seems to be moving toward a modicum of peace and prosperity.

I learn that Jan Masaryk, who had been foreign minister of Czechoslovakia's London-based government-in-exile during the war, is coming to New York to address the United Nations, and to visit his sister Alice. I also learn that he will be speaking at Columbia. Because of his connection to my family, I tell the news to my parents. They reply by asking me to approach him and deliver their greetings. But I am unwilling to do this.

"He has such great responsibilities," I say. "Why should he be bothered by someone like me?"

But my parents insist. And so, on the day of his address at a great hall at Columbia, I sit and listen, enthralled. Afterwards, as professors and students crowd around, trying to speak to him and ask questions, I hover in a corner, watching, listening.

After about forty minutes, the crowd finally disperses. Gathering my courage, I walk up to him shyly. I tell him who I am and relay greetings from my parents. Then comes a surprise.

Jan Masaryk opens his huge arms and holds me close. He asks me questions about both Mother and Father. I answer the best I can through my shyness. Then suddenly he asks, "Aničko, do you have a fountain pen?"

"No, I don't," I say. Fountain pens are a luxury. Without hesitation, he opens his jacket, pulls a Parker pen off the breast pocket of his shirt, and gives it to me. Then he kisses me with a smile, sends messages back to my parents, and says goodbye.

Adventure in Quebec

I am thrilled to receive the news that my friend Nan is transferring to Barnard to complete her B.A. I visit her in her room, and then I show her all I can of New York. She comes to dinner at our house as often as possible. As in our camp days, we have interesting experiences and get into our share of scrapes.

At Barnard, Nan takes a course in religion taught by Reinhold Niebuhr's wife, Ursula. When the Niebuhrs hold an "open house" for all their students, Nan takes me with her. Nan and I end up sitting on the floor close to Niebuhr's chair as he speaks with the students. It is a remarkable experience.

Nan is a year ahead of me. So after she graduates, she suggests that we take a trip together to Quebec for a week. It is late spring. We explore the Frontenac Castle, peer into art galleries and boutiques in Old Quebec, and ride the ferry on the St. Lawrence River. We walk the cobblestone streets that remind me of Prague. We practice our French.

On our last evening, we find ourselves in an elegant section, full of charming old houses and little shops. Suddenly both of us are very hungry. We are standing in front of a small restaurant with a menu posted at the entrance. All in French, with only a few words that we can recognize. So elegant, so mysterious. "Let's go," we say, and in we go. We are seated and served. We eat like queens.

But now the bill. Great Scott! We don't have enough money between us to cover the restaurant bill and get us home. We didn't notice that the menu posted outside had no prices. The owner arrives at our table, looking grave. We explain our situation, offer to wash dishes. Finally he accepts the money we can pay and lets us go with a severe warning. We rush out.

Outside the restaurant we hug each other and begin to laugh. We laugh with relief at our escape, and we laugh at our own naiveté. When we finally calm down, I remind Nan of the ridiculous song she sang at Camp Arden years earlier when we first met, and we burst into laughter once more. We laugh and giggle ourselves silly all the way home.

A Thank You Note for a Package to Prague

Dear Mrs. Baecher,
I have been thinking all week how to express my thanks for your precious gift, but most of all for the news that you are alive and that you have not forgotten us.

Today just these few lines with a thousand thanks and greetings to you and your loved ones. Your package arrived in perfect order at Tuzex. Everyone here wanted to look at the treasures you sent and even to have a little taste. But about this, I'll write in my next letter.

Today I remain, with heartfelt greetings and memories,
Always your Bohumila

CHAPTER 19

NEWS OF THE HOLOCAUST

Letters arrive from Prague more frequently now. Some come from my cousin Frank, who serves in the British Army and often makes trips to Prague, to see what he can learn, whom he can find. My parents write to him, send him packages of food, ask him to get them to relatives or friends they believe may still be in Prague. A few packages are received by those for whom they are intended. Most go undelivered.

Finally, the truth is clear. Most of our relatives on Father's side have been killed. My parents read the letters, and finally tell the news to me with sadness and tenderness: "Aničko, you need to know, my dear, that Uncle Leo and Aunt Miluska are no more."[1] I ask some questions and think about this and similar news with pain. It is hard to take in.

Just before Yom Kippur, Father surprises me by saying, "I am going to a synagogue for Yizkor services tomorrow, and

---

1   Leo and his wife were deported to Terezín in 1942, and were killed at Auschwitz in 1943.

you—" pointing at me, his Catholic daughter, "are coming with me." I am startled because Father never goes to religious services. He barely acknowledges his Jewish origins. And although my Catholicism is becoming less and less important to me, I know next to nothing about Judaism.

We go to Temple Emanu-El on Fifth Avenue. During the service the rabbi asks those who have lost family members during the past year to stand. Father stands up and I stand with him. I turn and see that the whole congregation is standing. Many are weeping. And then, thinking of my Uncle Leo, and all the other aunts, uncles, and cousins who did not escape when we did, remembering Mininka who played with me in Kácov and gave me those beautiful watercolors she painted to illustrate my fairy tales, I weep as well.

PART TWO

Remembrance and Return

1945–2012

CHAPTER 20

FAMILY REUNIONS

Once the war was over, borders between countries loosened up and travel became easier. People came to the United States, some to emigrate permanently, others to visit or connect with friends and family from whom they had been cut off. Some of these people were Holocaust survivors.

In my late teens at the time, I was much better informed about the disasters that had befallen European Jews than were most of my classmates. The concentration camps were a frequent topic of conversation at our dinner table. Father started to bring home copies of *Aufbau*, a publication designed for German-speaking Jewish refugees. In 1944, it started to provide names of survivors as well as victims, as information became available. Father studied the lists with great care and anxiety. From such sources, as well as from letters and phone calls, my parents knew more than many others of the terrible history that had affected the family.

There were many visitors from my extended family who came to New York. Among them was my father's cousin Karel, who had emigrated to Argentina; also the Nohels, whose situation was the concern of my grandmother's last correspondence from Prague. And there were Holocaust survivors. All were joyfully welcomed by my parents and our other New York-based relatives. Their experiences paralleled each other, although they wove through my life at different times. The first two survivors, Liselott Baecher and my Aunt Malva Schablin, rejoined our families when I was still in New York. The third was Paul Heller, a distant cousin who would play a large role in my later life.

The Princess of Roudnice

Liselott Baecher (later Liselott Fraenkl) was one of a kind. I think of her as I write this: elegant, witty, generous, totally alive. She was married to my father's cousin Pavel. While my father was born in Kácov, the village that became our summer home, his cousin grew up in Roudnice, a small manufacturing town not far from Prague.

Pavel's family developed a thriving business in farm

machinery. In their teens, two of my father's brothers were sent from Kácov to Roudnice to stay with their uncle, because the high school there – the gymnasium, as it was called – was better than the one in their home town.

When Pavel and Liselott were married, she was full of fun and pleasure, considered by her friends to be the "beautiful young princess of the whole town of Roudnice," as the executor of her will described her to my husband, Mark, and me years later, after her death.

Shortly before World War II broke out, the family scattered. Pavel's two older brothers emigrated to Rhodesia, now Zimbabwe, and to Argentina. Pavel, Liselott, and their daughter, Doris, stayed behind, for reasons that I never understood. In 1941, they were arrested by the Gestapo and ordered to report with their daughter to the train station the very next day. When they arrived, they recognized the whole Jewish community of Roudnice standing on the platform. All were loaded onto a train and transported to the ghetto in Lodz, Poland.

Temporary Survival in Lodz

In Lodz, the three Baechers were housed in a small room with three strangers – six people in all. Pavel was assigned to work in a smelting detail. The Germans needed a new smelting machine and, since Pavel was an engineer familiar with the work, they ordered him to build it. Of course he didn't have the right materials and they wouldn't provide them, but somehow he managed to use what was at hand and to perform the job.

In the meantime, Liselott repaired old uniforms. They were safe for the time being.

Then, in 1945, when the war was almost over, the Russian armies were advancing westward. Chaos everywhere. As the Russians came closer to Lodz, the Germans in charge of the ghetto decided to get out. The prisoners were given a choice: go west toward Germany, or stay and face their future with the Russians. Liselott and Pavel, who had in the meantime lost their daughter, chose to go west. Perhaps they feared that Pavel might be executed by the Russians as a former capitalist.

Contrary to Pavel's and Liselott's expectations, they were transported by train directly to the extermination camp in Auschwitz. Men and women were separated, and that was the last time that Pavel and Liselott saw each other. The women were sent by train to Breslau in Silesia, and then by forced march to yet another site in the Czech lands, a distance of about 100 miles.

Dirty Boots

During that march came a night in a freezing barn. Suddenly the door swung open, revealing a German officer holding up a pair of filthy boots. "Whoever cleans these boots to my satisfaction," he said, "will get this." He held up a slice of bread with his other hand.

"I will," called out Liselott, who was sitting near him. "But I need some shoe polish."

"Need?" sneered the German. "Where did you get this word 'need'? There is no such word here," and he slammed the door shut.

Liselott spent most of the night cleaning and polishing the boots, using spit, grass, and a bit of a rag she found in a corner of the barn. The next morning she got the bread and was strengthened for continuing the march.

When they arrived, the women were put on a cattle train and transported yet again to another notorious camp, Bergen-Belsen. Why this obsessive transportation of prisoners from camp to camp? Paul Heller would ask this question, others did as well. Didn't the Germans need resources such as coal and trains to continue the war? The answer is still not clear.

Close to Death

In Bergen-Belsen, Liselott was close to dying. That's when she was recognized by a fellow prisoner, Hana, who was a relative. Hana said, "I will help you. I will bring you food." She did. She brought Liselott boiled potatoes – an unheard of luxury to a concentration camp inmate – and Liselott gained some hope and some strength. Who knows where and how Hana got those potatoes. Telling this story later, Liselott said that throughout those years when things were at their worst, something or someone seemed to always turn up with help. It must be added that she always had the presence of mind to use that help as best she could.

When the war ended and the camp was liberated, a Swedish diplomat who later worked at the UN, Count Bernadotte, came to the camp. He issued a general invitation for any ex-prisoner who wanted to come to Sweden, to do so. Liselott was torn. Still unsure of Pavel's fate, she wanted to wait for him. But she also realized that in her condition she would be unable to be of use to him. And so she decided to go to Sweden.

Safe in Sweden

When Liselott arrived in Sweden she was admitted to a Red Cross hospital in Kalmar and given a bed with clean sheets. She had not seen sheets of any kind for four years. She spent most of her time in that hospital sleeping, cared for most tenderly by two Estonian women whom she didn't know and who didn't know her. They were drawn to Liselott by a special quality she had – whatever it was – that drew people to her throughout her life.

Liselott finally learned that her husband Pavel had died at Dachau. She accepted the news and went on.

Once a woman who recognized her came by and said: "What can I bring you?"

Liselott answered immediately, "Bring me a toothbrush and bring me a book." As she gained strength, Liselott came under the care of a Swedish doctor who was interested in restoring not only the ex-prisoners' physical health, but also their spiritual well being. This remarkable man would some-times suggest that Liselott and others go with him to a concert, a play, or a movie.

A Walk by Herself?

Liselott must have told the Swedish doctor in an early interview that she used to love to take long walks. And so, sometime later, he suggested that she take a walk outside the hospital, by herself. He took her to a door, opened it, said "Go," and shut the door behind her. She froze in place, unable to move. She couldn't do it. She turned around and returned, frightened, to the inside of the hospital. Later she tried again, and at that point she succeeded. She spoke about this to me years later, on a memorable walk we shared through Central Park in New York.

Liselott recovered. She came to New York. Her relatives in Scarsdale wanted her to come live with them, but she said that she needed to be independent. She set up a small dress-making business and designed and made the elegant outfits she herself wore when she was "the princess of Roudnice." She met a successful fabric designer, himself a refugee from Vienna. They married and that is how she became Liselott Fraenkl. They had a good life together. She lived to be over 100 years old.

Liselott was a frequent visitor to our New York home on West 72nd Street. Close to Malva – my second survivor – and to my parents, she told me once how generous they were to her when she needed help after arriving in America. She didn't go into detail, didn't need to.

Some years later, after my parents and Malva had died and I was married and living in Chicago, Liselott and I connected once again and became close friends. Whenever I came to New York, alone or with Mark and our young daughter,

117

Kathy, she and I would spend time together.

Liselott was aware of everything around her, responding with delight or anger at whatever was happening in the world. I recall her fury when Ed Koch, then Mayor of New York, cut the budget he had inherited from his predecessor. She was angry because he was hurting New York's school children, particularly the poor ones. A committed progressive, she followed presidential and congressional campaigns closely.

She once suggested that we start a book club between us. How, I asked. After all, we lived in two different cities. She was reading a book, she said, and when she would finish it she'd send it to me. I should do the same. We could then talk about these books over long distance telephone. The first book that she sent me was *84 Charing Cross Road*, by Helene Hanff, a book that was widely read at the time. Our book club lasted for several years.

A Late Spring Walk

I treasure one particular visit with Liselott. It was late spring. As usual, I stopped at the corner on East 74th Street to buy flowers from the Korean florist who had a small shop there, and up I went with them. When I arrived at her door, she greeted me and said, "It's so beautiful today, let's walk." And walk we did, across Manhattan, right through Central Park to the far end of West 72nd Street, passing the house overlooking the Hudson River where my family had lived for so many years. We talked the whole time.

Liselott spoke about the war and the concentration camps, which was rare for her. She said she valued Paul Heller's writing, and asserted that of all her readings on the subject, Heller and the Italian Primo Levi came closest to describing the way things really happened in those terrible dark days.

Suddenly she recalled her inability to take that solitary walk from the Swedish hospital. She stopped walking, stood still, and looked at me very directly with her deep blue eyes. "You know, Aničko," she said, as close as I can remember, "You need to understand this. When they imprisoned us, even when they didn't kill us right away, they did their best to destroy our spirits. They wanted us to lose hope, to be afraid, to stamp out our own sense of freedom. They almost succeeded with me, when I was too frightened to walk alone outside that hospital. But finally I managed it."

Then that subject was closed and she asked probing questions about our life in Chicago, about Mark, about our girls, about my brothers and their children. And we talked of books and, of course, politics. Finally we stopped for lunch at the café I loved so much as a young girl newly arrived in New York, The Éclair. Its walls were still papered with foreign newspapers and the chatter was still a mix of many tongues. For dessert, of course, we each had an éclair.

Malva Baecher Schablin

CHAPTER 21

MALVA AND HER VISITORS

In the fall of 1946, my father returned to Prague to see if anyone else in the family had survived. He knew that the Nessys were not in danger; he had connected with some of them earlier. Among the Baechers he found one person, his sister Malvina, or Malva. She was the closest Holocaust survivor in my life.

Malva had spent the last two years of the war in Terezín, a "transition camp" from which people were eventually transported to death camps further east. Many died in Terezín from disease, starvation, or torture, but there were no gas chambers there. Malva's entire family – her son Willi, daughter Eva, their spouses, and Malva's beloved granddaughter, Janinka – were all transported from Terezín and gassed at Auschwitz.

Malva survived, against her own wishes. She told me once of walking in the streets of Terezín while all the others, prisoners and guards alike, were hiding because Allied bombers were rumbling overhead. "Here! Here!" she wanted to call out, to have bombs dropped on Terezín, to destroy her as well as everyone and everything in it. But it didn't happen, and she and others survived.

My Second Mother

When my father and she were reunited in Prague, he begged Malva to come to America to live with us. He was a very persuasive man. At first she refused, saying she needed to stay in Prague with some of the other survivors. But finally she agreed.

When she arrived at New York harbor and all of us were there to welcome her, she pointed to me, smiled, and said, "You will be my girl." That is how in my late teens I had the astonishing experience of being loved and nurtured by two completely different women, who, at the same time, accepted and loved each other as well as me. I grew into adulthood with two mothers.

Before she arrived, I was nervous because I thought I remembered Malva from Europe as a little fierce, and somewhat scary. When I came to know her in New York, she wasn't like that at all. Perhaps my memory was wrong; perhaps suffering had changed her.

Malva looked much like her mother – the grandmother I adored in my early years in Prague, who died in her bed before the terrible transports began. Slight, with dark hair, she wore black skirts and white blouses, always. A determined atheist, she smiled at the confusing glimmers of Christianity and Judaism that occasionally mingled in our family affairs.

Smoking, Baking, Joking

Malva's beautiful Czech speech was sometimes peppered with German or Yiddish phrases, especially when she wanted to make a particular point. She knew many jokes and told them often, saying that humor and laughter had kept her and her friends sane in the stark, bizarre atmosphere of Terezín.

Malva was a non-stop smoker, and this was difficult for my singer mother. Eventually Julia accepted Malva's smoking with the generosity that was part of her nature. "After all, I'm no longer a performer," she said. "I can now live with the cigarettes." But she was unhappy later, when I picked up Malva's smoking habit. She tried very hard to make me stop, though I didn't give it up for many years.

Malva didn't go with us to concerts or plays. She said that her daughter Eva had been devoted to the arts and that sitting in a theater or concert hall would bring memories too painful to bear. Her pleasures were different from ours. She loved to cook and, like her mother, was a great baker. And she was very social, spending much time with friends – in person, on the telephone, or through letters. She kept up a lively correspondence from America with her fellow survivors, who had scattered to England, Canada, Israel, and even Kenya.

Malva's Court

After her arrival, we had many visitors. Her brother, my Uncle Benno, lived nearby and came almost every day. But most of her visitors were women. Eventually, a kind of court developed around Malva. Several of her visitors worked at Radio Free Europe or Voice of America during the war. Others were translators at the newly-formed Czech embassy. There was a doctor, a dentist, and two salesladies from Saks Fifth Avenue.

A frequent visitor was Joan Winn. We called her Hanka. She was the wife of a psychiatrist and the mother of two daughters who became well-known writers later on. Hanka was warm, generous, and I loved her. A close friend of Hanka's, Dr. Ella Traub, lived in Hanka's building. She was the personal physician to many in the Czech émigré community, including Alice Masaryk and my Malva.

Hanka volunteered at Amnesty International almost every day, calling this organization her "last love." In addition to Malva, Hanka had an army of friends, including Liselott. Years later, when my parents and Malva were gone, I often stayed with Hanka when I visited New York from Chicago.

Most of Malva's early visitors were daughters of other Holocaust victims. She had been their mothers' friend in Europe, and these women, who had escaped Prague the way we did, were reaching for a connection to their dead parents. They came almost daily – sometimes just one or two, at other times a larger group.

Reenacting The Past

Years before, Malva had sat with their mothers at small tables in Prague cafés, drinking coffee, eating pastries, smoking and chatting about the events of the day. Now Malva's visitors sat with her at the round coffee table in our living room, in an unconscious re-enactment of those earlier café meetings. They drank coffee, ate Malva's delicious pastries, and talked and listened. What they wanted was to be with Malva, to hear about life during the war, about their own parents, about Terezín.

Malva did not speak much about her wartime suffering, but all of us were aware of it. Once she talked about the visit to Terezín by the Swiss Red Cross in June 1944, when the Nazis wanted to demonstrate to inspectors from the International Red Cross how well Hitler treated "his" Jews.

Scornfully, Malva spoke of how easily the visitors were duped. They never noticed, she said, that the healthy-looking children who marched in front of the inspectors several times during the day were always the same ones – probably recent arrivals at the camp. And none of the inspectors tried to run water into the sinks in the bathrooms. They would have been surprised to see that no water ran out of the gleaming faucets. "It was all an ugly charade," said Malva, with a rough laugh, "but at least we had a good meal that day."

My mother was never part of these visits, nor was I. My time with Malva came later. I would sit on her bed in the evening, and we'd talk. Sometimes we talked about ordinary happenings of the day. She was interested in all aspects of contemporary life in America, and she was particularly delighted with the new household conveniences that were available here, now that the war was over. I recall her pleasure in electric mixers and toasters, as well as homely things such as Kleenex, paper towels, and Brillo. Then sometimes a sudden recollection from the terrible past would, like distant thunder, flash across her face.

Once she told me a story about a young woman, a distant relative of ours, who was despised by other female prisoners because she was too sexy, too friendly with the dreaded guards. "She was a good person," Malva said with sudden passion. "Her work duty was in the fruit orchard. She could have been shot if they had caught her stealing any of the fruit, but once she took a chance. She stole an apple, hid it in her clothes, and gave it to Janinka for her birthday. I'll never forget her." I like to think this was Hana, the same relative who brought potatoes to Liselott in Bergen-Belsen and helped her survive.

Faithful Listeners

I think Malva told such stories to me because she knew that, for some reason, I was able to listen quietly, without dramatics. At other times *I* did the talking, and Malva listened to me with great attention, even respect, commenting on my teenage concerns about school, clothes, homework, and boyfriends. Perhaps my stories reminded her of similar talks she had once held with her daughter Eva.

Malva, like Liselott, was deeply involved in the life around her. Her delight in dishwashers, mixers, and paper towels was similar to Liselott's investment in the New York schools and police system. It was clear to me from the beginning that focusing on the world around them gave them both rich new lives.

My Mother's Projects

In contrast to Malva, my mother kept busy with duty and work. She did find time for me. We went to movies and museums together, and I was always aware of her concern and love. But she was not comfortable with sitting down to a cup of coffee and casual conversation with acquaintances for more than ten minutes. Instead, she loved to teach. One of her favorite students was Caroline, the wife of my cousin Ivan. She spent time transposing music from voice or piano to harp, and pursuing various cultural projects. Her friends were fellow musicians who shared her interests.

One of the major projects undertaken by Julia Nessy and Alice Masaryk: The creation and placement of a bust of Antonin Dvořák, by Croatian sculptor Ivan Meštrović, in Lincoln Center, New York. Julia Nessy, 2nd from left. Alice Masaryk, in hat, far right, with members of the Czech-American community.

A collaborator on many of her projects, including some ambitious concerts, was Alice Masaryk. The two of them often worked together in organizing cultural events. Fortunately, our apartment was large enough to accommodate both Mother and Malva, with their different tastes and lifestyles.

From left: Alice Backer, Frank Backer, Julia Nessy, Anna Nessy Perlberg, Paul Backer, Liselott Fraenkl

Mother worried that Malva's stories would fill me with depression and negativity, but she need not have worried. For one thing, she herself provided a helpful counter-influence. There was laughter in our home and the sound of folk songs. My mother knew many of these – Czech, Slovak, even some Hungarian ones – and my brothers and I learned many of them from her. I loved them all.

CHAPTER 22

LOVE, MARRIAGE, TOKYO, AND GOODBYES

My closeness with Malva became a great boon in 1949, when my father suffered a major stroke from which he never recovered. It was now my mother's turn to be the caregiver, the nurse, and she devoted herself completely to the task. The folk songs dwindled down to just a few. Our home became a very sad place. Malva held the family together with her powerful personality, her humor, and her love. Perhaps we were now her family in yet another sense, succeeding the family she had lost.

My brothers focused their energies on study, and both did graduate work at Columbia. Charlie became a lawyer, Paul a mathematician. They met two young women who were refugees like themselves; their weddings were two days apart. Charlie married Ellen Wolf and had a daughter, Carol, and two sons, Steven and David. Paul married Charlotte Drews and had a son, Tom, and a daughter, Susan. The two families remained in the New York area and were together frequently.

After graduating from Barnard, I did graduate work in history at Columbia. That is how I met Mark Perlberg, who was a graduate student in English.

Mark and I would sit in front of the stone lions that guarded Columbia's Low Library and we'd talk of politics and literature. I fell in love with his humor and his knowledge of literature, his talk of Yeats and Auden and Dylan Thomas. He fell in love with my passion for politics and what he called my foreignness – even, he said, the rough dark bread of the sandwiches I brought from home for lunch. It was so different from his family's soft white bread.

After I earned my master's degree, I went to teach at a girls' school in Connecticut, and he often visited me there. I was surprised when he impulsively quit graduate school and let himself be drafted. The Korean War had just begun. Now our roles reversed, and I visited him where he was stationed near Augusta, Georgia. When he finished basic training, he called to tell me that he would have a leave of two weeks. Would I marry him during that time? I said yes.

A Small Wedding

We were married by a judge in his New York chambers. He was Mark's uncle, so the event was as personal as we could make it. By now my father's illness was in its fourth year. He and I walked together to the ceremony, Father walking slowly, painfully hanging onto my arm. From time to time we would look at each other and smile. Father's mouth was crooked from the stroke, but his bearing was as proud and dignified as ever.

And then the small reception in our 72nd Street apartment overlooking the Hudson River. True to their characters, my mother worried about my wardrobe and filled the whole apartment with flowers, while Malva took three days to create my gorgeous wedding cake.

Anna's father escorting her to her wedding

Anna and her father

*Anna's "two mothers," Julia and Malva, leaving for Anna's wedding
(Anna is in the background)*

As we and our closest relatives sat down at the reception after the marriage ceremony, my Uncle Benno, Malva's and Father's brother, stood up and said he would say a few words in place of his brother, who was unable to speak. Everything had happened so quickly, we had not even thought to ask him. Addressing Mark's relatives, Benno spoke about our emigration from Czechoslovakia, our family's experiences, my father's struggle to build a new life. He spoke lovingly about me and said how much his brother would wish for my and Mark's future. I have never forgotten his words. I will always be deeply grateful to him for this beautiful gesture.

Then we sat down to the formal lunch. I looked to the kitchen entrance and saw our Mary Goetz, who had cared for my family, cooked, cleaned, and worried for us all for so many years. Smiling, she held up her champagne glass in a silent toast to me, and I jumped up and ran to the kitchen, where we embraced.

Anna and Mark enjoying their wedding reception

After our brief honeymoon, Mark reported for duty and I returned to teaching at my school. Mark was sent to Korea. We wrote to each other often, had a few phone conversations, but the separation was hard to take. Then a surprising event. Mark was recalled from Korea to Tokyo to work for *Stars and Stripes*, the Army newspaper. He called to ask me whether I would join him. I agreed.

Mark in Korea

Another Leaving

And so there was another farewell. Goodbye to New York. Goodbye to my sick father, my two mothers. We were at the start of another great new adventure. Mark and I lived in a Japanese house, talked politics with Tokyo neighbors, explored Japanese pottery, woodblock prints, and literature. Mark carried a small notebook with him to sketch out ideas for poems wherever we went. Traces of our Asian experience glimmered in his poems for the rest of his life.

A New Home

After my arrival in Tokyo, we spent two days in the Imperial Hotel designed by Frank Lloyd Wright. I recall the elegant wooden paneling, the tall beams, the scrolls hanging on the walls. It was wonderful to be there.

On the third day, Mark took me to see the home he had rented for us. We took a train to Toritsu Daigaku, a suburb on the outskirts of the city. We would live Japanese style in one half of a house. With smiles and much bowing, we met the owners, a man, his wife and little girl, Atsuko-chan, and his mother, the *obasan*. They lived in the other half of the house. We entered the outer hall, took off our shoes as instructed, and entered our living area.

Soft straw (*tatami*) floors, sliding doors (*shoji*) to open or close off spaces. The cooking facilities consisted of a single burner gas-range, a sink, and some storage space. The landlord showed us the bathroom and explained that the purpose of the bathtub (*ofuro*) was for peace and relaxation. One was to enter it only after washing and cleaning oneself on the wooden planks outside the tub. It was used only once a week. I had much to learn.

Atsuko-chan

I loved little Atsuko-chan. About five years old, she would come to visit our part of the house from time to time. We gave each other language lessons. She would walk around the room, point to something, and pronounce its Japanese name. I would repeat it after her as best I could, and then say its English equivalent: "table," perhaps. She would repeat after me. She even taught me a little song asking the spring to come quickly because then she could wear the pretty pink clogs meant for little girls to wear at that time of year.

Explorations, Kyoto

We traveled every chance we had. The highlight was a trip to Kyoto. A Japanese colleague of Mark's, Mr. Kano, gave him a card with many characters written on it. He said to take a cab from the train station, show the card to the driver, and then upon arrival at the place give the card to the proprietor.

We followed his instructions, but the cab driver had difficulties finding the place. He asked directions several times. Finally he said, "Ah, Nijo Jinya." He dropped us off, we entered the place, and were told to wait in a side room. Light gold tatami on the floor, a scroll depicting a mountain rising in a mist, three men in a boat. Then a soft-spoken young woman in a light blue kimono entered and asked us in a silvery voice: "You look? You stay?" She was asking whether we were planning to simply visit and look around or to actually stay there. We answered: "We stay, if you allow." She disappeared again, then brought us tea.

Nijo-Jinya

That evening we were taken to our room. White walls, beautifully carved bare wood beams, wood and paper shoji marking off the boundaries of the room, soft woven-straw tatami, our brown and beige futons prepared for us to sleep. When we pulled back a sliding door, we saw that the room had a small private garden with its own stone fountain. Sandy ground, five stones of varying size, a few pines. It was hard to leave the room in the morning, but when we did, we were served breakfast: two fried eggs and rice – to be eaten with chopsticks. We didn't manage it very gracefully.

There were two young men in the hallway as we prepared to leave for a day's sightseeing. They introduced themselves and said they were students, learning English. They would take turns showing us their Kyoto, today one, the next day the other. They wanted to practice their English.

We learned from them that staying at Nijo Jinya was a great privilege. We were the first Americans to stay there – ever. The place had served as secret housing for nobles coming to Kyoto to visit the shogun who lived in the Nijo-jo, the great palace nearby, from which the shogun ruled.

With the help of the two young men, we visited that

palace and some of the great temples of the city. We also saw one of the rock gardens of a Zen monastery. Designed to aid meditation, it was composed of rocks, moss, a few pines and sand to represent water. As we approached, it was being tended by a monk with a broom-like implement. We received the greatest honor when one of the young men took us to meet the family of his fiancée. We drank tea and chatted with his future in-laws.

Sipping Tea As The Moon Rises

The next day the second young man took us to visit a well-known potter. We went by bus to his village and called at his workshop where he showed us some of his work. I remember how he gently placed delicate, rose-colored cups on the table, saying that their purpose was for sipping tea while watching the moon rise on a fall evening. Then he led us to his brick-lined kiln, which was located in a nearby shack. I recall his rapid walk, his kimono slapping against the shanks of his legs as he strode ahead of us.

When we returned to Tokyo, Mark and I talked about the contrast between our landlords and the friendly, generous people we had just met in Kyoto. Our relationship with our landlords was becoming more and more difficult. The lady of the house, the obasan, was the widow of a man who had held a high rank in the Japanese military that had occupied Manchuria during the early part of Japan's invasion of China, years before. She was unfriendly to us, clearly not delighted to have American barbarians living in her home. Her son, on the other hand, was a radical leftist, perhaps a Communist. In those awful days of red-baiting in the United States, he was convinced that all Americans loved Joe McCarthy. He would visit our part of the house periodically and quiz us, full of accusation and hostility. We finally decided that we should move.

Cherry Blossoms and Firebombs

We answered an ad and took a train to meet a woman who might possibly become our new landlord. Descending the stairs at the train station, we saw a very old lady wearing a yellow and brown kimono, a beautiful yellow *obi* (sash), and holding an elegant parasol. Her English was excellent.

She told us that years before, she had visited Washington D.C., as a member of the Japanese delegation that brought the gift of cherry trees from the Japanese people to the United States – the same trees that are today a beautiful landmark of our capital. Later, she spoke of her experience in the Tokyo firebombing. There were fires everywhere, she said, including her own neighborhood. She ran in every direction, and each time, it seemed, she would be met by advancing flames. Finally she ran into a large cemetery, fell down exhausted on top of a grave, held onto the stone. "Very well," she thought, "this is where I will stop. I will either live or die, whatever my fate is."

She lived, her home burned to cinders, her family and most of her neighbors dead. But she lived.

Her home was too big and too expensive for us, so we reluctantly turned it down and returned home. Heartbroken by her story, we stopped looking for a new place. Perhaps, like she, we were thinking, "So, living with these difficult people may be our fate. We will stay."

Goodbye to Japan

In 1954, Mark's tour of duty ended. He was being discharged and we would be transported to the States. We felt unsure of the future because the Japanese experience had been so rich, so all-encompassing. But other riches were awaiting us. As our ship moved toward land in the evening, the Seattle harbor seemed to be embraced by a perfect necklace of gorgeous diamond lights, welcoming us home.

After a few days of exploring Mount Rainier National Park, we flew to New York and were welcomed by both of our families. Mother told us that Father's condition had been in decline for several months. He now rarely left his bed, even with help. He needed to have someone with him at all times. When we reached our apartment, I ran to his room, to his bed. He gave me a soft, crooked smile of welcome, but that was all. I saw that he was greatly diminished.

Two More Goodbyes

My father died on April 30, 1956. Mother had been spending almost all her waking hours sitting by his side. She had a nurse as well, to help with some of his physical needs, but she rarely left him. I, too, sat with him often, holding his hand. My brothers did the same. On that evening, Mother sat with me and Malva in the kitchen, taking a bit of rest. And that was when the nurse came in and told her that Father was gone. Mother was beside herself. She couldn't bear the thought that she hadn't been with him. "Why didn't you come for me? Why didn't you call me?" She was heartbroken that they weren't together at his final moment.

As he had requested, we held a modest Jewish funeral. We were all there: Mother, Mark and I, my brothers, Charlie's wife, Ellen, Paul's wife, Charlotte, Malva, Benno, Father's business partner, a few neighbors and friends. Alice Masaryk, now a very old lady, came and laid a single red rose on Father's coffin. After the Kaddish, my mother reached for my hand and the two of us whispered the Lord's Prayer together – in Czech.

Malva died two years later, of cancer. I was flying in to see her, but I arrived too late. I was told that at the end her doctor, our friend Ella Traub, left her room with tears streaming down her face. Malva was cremated, as she wanted. I don't remember the memorial, though I know there was one and I was there. Her ashes lie close to her brother's. The pain of losing these two loves of mine was hard.

Some months after Malva's death, Mother closed up the apartment at 344 West 72nd Street, the address that had been our home for so many years. She made a surprising connection with the architect who had remodeled our Prague house years ago, and who had also emigrated to the United States just before World War II broke out.

Now he agreed to design and build a small house for her on my brother Paul's property in Yorktown Heights, in Westchester County, New York. All on one level, it had a living room, bedroom, bath, and small kitchenette. It was too small for the grand piano from our old apartment, so Paul and his wife Charlotte moved it into their house. Mother bought an upright piano, and there was room for her harp. She would continue a little teaching and other activities as well as she could. It seemed as if our house in Prague had sent a small offspring to look after her.

CHAPTER 23

A NEW LIFE ONCE MORE: CHICAGO

After Mark's discharge from the Army and our return to the U.S., his job hunt was difficult. He interviewed with the editors of literary journals, but found that most of them were more interested in his poetry than in his journalism. One editor actually took a poem for publication in the same letter in which he rejected Mark's job application. But finally, after about a year, he was hired by *Time*.

Mark at TIME

Things were a bit easier for me. I was hired by the publisher Knopf to a lowly but interesting position. I teamed up with a friend from Barnard, and I thoroughly enjoyed seeing great literary people come into the office to see Alfred and Blanche Knopf. My eyes popped when I saw the poet Wallace Stevens and later, the great German novelist Thomas Mann.

Then, in 1956, *Time* assigned Mark to its Chicago bureau. We had to move. We bought a used car, piled in our belongings, including our scruffy dog Petey, and drove west. When we saw the tall stacks of Gary, Indiana, puffing out huge streams of gray smoke, we knew we were in for something new, something different. We arrived in Chicago, were welcomed by the *Time* bureau chief, and wondered about what was to come.

Anna and Mark

Children

Our first daughter, Katherine, was born in September, 1957. We called her Kathy then, but today she is Kate. Our second daughter, Julie, followed in 1960.

Caring for our girls was very special to me. Having been raised by governesses whose chief concerns seemed to be keeping my face, hands, and nails clean, my clothing and table manners proper, and my speech polite and socially acceptable, I wanted the

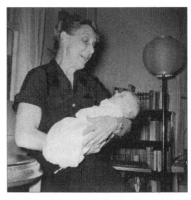

Julia singing to baby Kathy, 1957

opposite for Kathy and Julie. I enjoyed their games with friends and with each other. Julie whispered stories to our now elderly dog, Petey, much the way I had whispered stories to my doll Suzanka years before.

Mark and I loved our daughters' discoveries of the world. Mark never forgot seeing Kathy standing full of wonder at our living room window after a snowy Chicago night, staring out and saying: "Look, the color is gone." And Julie, as she heard birds twittering around us, saying "the trees are talking." Some

Mark, Anna, and baby Kathy

of their sayings found their way into Mark's poems.

Once I took them to the Lincoln Park Zoo to look at a new exhibit of exotic birds. They looked seriously, but without much interest. But as we exited the zoo, they spotted a nest that some swallows had built high up within the passageway. Kathy and Julie kept looking up, excited. They would not move. One of them said: "These are *real* birds."

When they started school, first Kathy, then Julie, I worried, hoped, and questioned every possible thing. They finished middle and high school at an excellent private institution in Chicago. They went on to college, Kate to Oberlin in Ohio, Julie to Pitzer in California. They married happily, developed careers, had children, and as their children were growing up, they worried, hoped and questioned in turn, and we with them.

Journalism and The Poetry Center of Chicago

Mark's beat at *Time* was business and the arts. He loved to interview musicians – Renata Tebaldi, Fritz Reiner. He came to know Studs Terkel and Nelson Algren. When Jack Kennedy traveled around the Midwest to begin prospecting for the presidency, Mark, together with other reporters, traveled with him. He loved it all.

After Mark left *Time*, he went on to freelance and work for *World Book*, *Encyclopædia Britannica*, *Prism*, and Rotary International. All the while, he continued to write poems, and he published more and more in literary journals. In 1970, William Morrow published his first book of poems, *The Burning Field*.

In 1973, Paul Carroll, a Chicago poet and friend of Mark's, convened a meeting of several Chicago poets. His purpose was to establish a center for poetry readings at a location that would be accessible to the general public. This was the beginning of The Poetry Center of Chicago. Chicago's Museum of Contemporary Arts was the Center's first home, and Paul was its first president. Eventually, Paul moved on to other things and the presidency was taken over by other poets, including Mark, who held the position for several years. Eventually, I was invited to join the board as well.

Over a period of some 30 years, The Poetry Center brought international, national, and local poets and prose writers to read to Chicago audiences and to interact with them. Among its many readers were Allen Ginsberg, W. S. Merwin, Gwendolyn Brooks, Sir Stephen Spender, Billy Collins, Lawrence Ferlinghetti, William Stafford, Lisel Mueller; prose writers were Saul Bellow, John Cheever, Grace Paley, Patricia Hampl. Joseph Brodsky and Derek Walcott read at the Poetry Center long before they won their Nobel Prizes for Literature, and the Polish Nobel Laureate Czeslaw Milosz read twice.

Teaching On Two Fronts

While reporting for *Time* and later, editing for other publications, Mark began to teach a poetry workshop at the Newberry Library of Chicago. He loved teaching, and found new friends among some of his students.

As for me, I was caring for our girls. When they were

Anna at the Bowman Center

older, I worked as director of social rehabilitation programs for the Bowman Center at Chicago's Rush Medical Center. But while they were still young, I started teaching an introductory evening course in political science at the Illinois Institute of Technology. In the course, we read and discussed speeches and writings by civil rights leaders, as well as material on civil disobedience by Henry David Thoreau and Martin Luther King.

Most of the students were policemen who took the course to satisfy requirements for advancement on the force. At the end of the course, one student told me that he enjoyed the course so much that he had changed his major – to political science. Later, I hoped that none of my students took part in the "police riot" that accompanied the Democratic Convention of 1968. Perhaps that was too much to hope for.

Political Action

The political upheavals of the time changed us. When, in the latter part of 1967, Senator Eugene McCarthy of Minnesota announced that he would challenge President Johnson for the Democratic presidential nomination, we joined his following. The organizer for McCarthy in Illinois was Dick Simpson, a progressive Texan who taught at the University of Illinois-Chicago Campus. Dick recruited us, our neighbors and friends, as well as many others to work in the McCarthy campaign.

That is when I learned to ring doorbells and speak to strangers about politics. This did not come naturally to me, but finally it became easier. I recalled overhearing those long-ago conversations Father had had with Alfred Baker Lewis; somehow that helped. And I thought my grandmother Anna Nessy, who had demonstrated for the rights of political prisoners in Prague, would have approved.

CHAPTER 24

MORE WARTIME MEMORIES

In the background, and sometimes the foreground, of our life in Chicago, the Holocaust continued to be a powerful presence. I connected with my cousin Paul Heller, whom I had met only briefly years before when he first arrived in New York, on his way to a great career in medicine. That career brought him to Chicago where we became friends and I learned his survival story from him and his writings.

I also found a close friend in Marjánka Fousková, who had been a childhood playmate of my cousin Ivan in Prague. Daughter of a Jewish mother and a Christian father, she had spent the war years in Prague. From her I learned about the humiliations meted out to "half-Jewish" children such as she in those dark years. My story would have been the same, had we not fled when we did.

And I met Eva Lutovsky, who had helped her mother hide Jews and political dissidents from the Gestapo in their small suburban house while her mother held down a daytime job being the secretary of the puppet president of the country, Emil Hácha.

All these encounters were profoundly important, but it was Paul's friendship and his story that made the most powerful impression on me.

Dr. Paul Heller

Paul Heller

At the very beginning of our adventure in Chicago, on the very day we arrived, a box of chocolates was waiting for us in our hotel room. We opened it. It was a gift from Paul and his wife Liese. With this delicious welcome, we no longer felt so alone in the big new city.

Soon we were invited to dinner at the Hellers' and were treated with great kindness and warmth. We now had family in Chicago! I was familiar with most of Paul's horrific past experiences, but now they became more real to me. He gave me a copy of the article he had published in *Midstream* telling his story.

Paul was a distant cousin of ours, born at the start of World War I in Komotau, a city in the Sudetenland. Komotau was just five miles from the Sudeten Mountains that formed the border between Germany and what became Czechoslovakia after 1918. The culture in the Sudetenland was German and remained so even after the dissolution of the Austrian Empire, when only a few Czechs moved into the area. There was little social mixing between the Germans and the Czechs. We were related to the Hellers through my grandmother, Wilhelmina Baecher, who was a cousin of Paul's father.

Early on, Paul decided that medicine would be his calling. His father had been a physician, and perhaps his mother's leukemia turned Paul's interest to hematology. Together with his older brother Erich, Paul grew up in a highly cultured German milieu, at the center of which was devotion to German literature and music.

I don't think either Paul or Erich had much

communication with the Baechers, even when they came to live in Prague (1933-1936), fleeing the Nazi plague that was spreading from Germany. They had a strong social circle of their own, friends from the past who had also moved to Prague as the Nazis gained strength in Germany. Erich eventually moved farther away to England, and Paul became engrossed in medical studies.

Paul's story has a heartbreaking irony to it. As a young medical student, he waited to emigrate when others were leaving because he wanted to earn his medical certification before leaving Prague. Arrested for political activity, he was ordered to leave the country. But his plane ticket to England, dated September 4, 1939, turned out to be worthless because World War II had broken out just days before. Paul was arrested again, and this time sent to Buchenwald. This was the beginning of the six years he spent in concentration camps. He survived through luck, random chance, and extraordinary spirit.

After four years in Buchenwald, where he suffered the usual concentration camp experience of hard labor and starvation, Paul was transferred to Auschwitz. Why? Reasons were never given, never known. In Auschwitz he was assigned to work in a quarry, to shovel, carry, and break very heavy stones. He developed severe pain in the back of his neck. Because of his medical training, he recognized his condition as a fractured vertebra, the "shoveler's fracture" which was known to occur to miners.

Reporting to the prison clinic was dangerous; it usually led to death. But Paul's pain was so severe that he took the risk and described his symptoms to the German doctor in charge. By sheer luck, this doctor recognized Paul's symptoms as a case of "shoveler's fracture" because he had specialized in the condition, had written a paper about it, and was very interested in its outcome. He admitted Paul to the clinic, and Paul's life was spared.

Later, Paul was assigned to be a doctor at a small branch camp of Auschwitz called Jaworzno. Even the worst camps had doctors, usually Jews, perhaps because those in charge were afraid that if severe contagion was involved, it might affect them as well as the prisoners.

Toward the end of the war, as the Russian army advanced toward Germany, the commanders of Paul's camp decided to evacuate and force-march the prisoners westward. This was one of the famous "death marches." Paul called them "the crowning torture in the lives of the prisoners."[1] They marched endlessly, it seemed, from Jaworzno to another camp called Gross-Rosen. Next, they were transported by freight train back to Buchenwald, the site of Paul's first imprisonment. But Buchenwald was already overrun by prisoners who had been evacuated from other camps before the advance of western Allies. Paul wrote, "The chaos of those days brought death to many prisoners. When the SS fled on April 11, 1945, many of the 21,000 survivors were incapable of rising from their mattresses to celebrate the occasion."

During the march from Jaworzno toward Gross-Rosen, Paul thought about dying. He debated with himself and

---

1   This and the following quotes are from Paul Heller's "A Concentration Camp Diary," published in *Midstream*, April 1980, pp. 29-36.

recorded these debates in a diary he kept on the pages of an old farmer's calendar. He wrote every three or four days, whenever he found an opportunity. "It might be beautiful to lie down tonight in the straw and to give up," he wrote. Then he answered himself, "No, this cannot be, Freedom is perhaps closer than you believe. Do you know what freedom is?… Yes, remember. There is joy, work of your choice, love, home, people without uniforms, books, music, helping others. … I am grateful for these encouragements from the depth of my soul."

Paul began recalling passages from Goethe's *Faust* that he had learned years earlier in school, and he kept reciting them to himself: "I feel my powers loftier, clearer, I glow as drunk with new made wine, my heart has strength to face the world again."[2] He recited these words over and over, the rhythm of the poem keeping pace with his steps, and he marched on, all the way to Buchenwald.

When Edward R. Murrow came to Buchenwald with the liberating American Army, he asked a guard if he could meet a former prisoner. He was told, "Well, there is a young doctor." That was Paul. He and a French physician showed Murrow around. They spent the day together. As they walked, children drew near to touch Murrow, and a man dropped dead as he and the doctors walked by.

When saying goodbye, Murrow asked Paul, "Is there anything I can do for you?" Paul answered, "Let my brother

---

2   Ibid. Paul Heller states that the quote from Goethe's *Faust* is from the Bayard Taylor translation, edited by Stuart Atkins.

know that I am alive." And so, in Murrow's next broadcast, he began, "Permit me to tell you what you would have seen, and heard, had you been with me on Thursday. It will not be pleasant listening. If you are at lunch, or if you have no appetite to hear what Germans have done, now is a good time to switch off the radio, for I propose to tell you of Buchenwald." He described the conditions in the barrack which was occupied by Czechoslovaks, 1200 men in a building built to stable 80 horses.

"The stink was beyond all description.... I asked how many men had died in that building during the last month. They called the doctor. We inspected his records.... Behind the names of those who had died, there was a cross. I counted them. They totaled 242 – 242 out of 1200, in one month. As I walked down to the end of the barracks, there was applause from the men too weak to get out of bed. It sounded like the handclapping of babies, they were so weak. The doctor's name was Paul Heller."[3]

Paul's brother, Erich, heard the broadcast and flew from Cambridge, England to a tearful reunion. Eventually Paul came to the U.S. with help from Murrow and others. That is how we met him briefly in New York.

Paul went on to marry his love, Liese Florsheim, and return to his life's calling in medicine. His work took him from New York to Washington D.C., Omaha, and then Chicago, to the Department of Hematology at the College of

---

3   The transcript of Edward R. Murrow's "Broadcast from Buchenwald" (April 15, 1945) can be found in *In Search of Light: The Broadcasts of Edward R. Murrow, 1938-1961*, New York, Alfred A. Knopf, 1967.

Medicine, University of Illinois, where he was teaching and doing research when we arrived in Chicago. There he made great contributions in the fight against sickle cell anemia.

When a child in our family was diagnosed with a severe illness, Paul couldn't do enough to help. He gave advice, contacts, people to call, things to avoid.

Paul loved music all his life. He told me early on that he had heard two of my mother's concerts in Prague and had loved them. That meant a great deal to me. Paul, Liese, Mark and I went to several concerts together, some at Ravinia, a summer festival site north of Chicago.

After Liese's death from cancer, Paul married another Holocaust survivor, Anna Novak. We began to identify ourselves on the telephone: "This is the other Anna." Paul and Anna met us frequently for lunch at a Japanese restaurant in Evanston. As his hearing diminished, it was important to find places where the background noise would not be too great. Our conversations were often about politics and music, and we happily agreed on most things: who was conducting currently, who were the soloists the conductor used. He rarely talked of his past, but when asked a direct question about a specific detail, he would answer readily. That is how he came to send me a copy of his autobiographical manuscript: "Autobiographic Sketches: The First Forty Years."

Over the years, I had many telephone conversations with Paul. I loved hearing his deep baritone voice, as he ended our conversations every time with "All the best. All the best."

When Paul died in 2001, I was honored to be asked to speak on behalf of our scattered family at his memorial service. The place was crowded with his colleagues and former students from the University of Illinois. All wanted to pay tribute to him for his great accomplishments in medicine, as well as his great qualities as a human being.

Marjánka Fousková

Marjánka Fousková was, like me, the daughter of one Jewish and one Catholic parent. She had known some members of my family as a small child and had played with my cousin Ivan. Her Jewish mother was transported to Terezín, the "transition camp," where – through happenstance and good fortune – she stayed alive, avoiding the transports to death camps in the east.

Marjánka, who was a year younger than I, was not sent to Terezín. Instead, she was allowed to stay in Prague with her father. As a "half-Jewish" girl, she could not attend school, go to the movies, ride the tram, play in the park. The only place in which she and others like her could play safely was the old cemetery in the Jewish section of the city. I have an image of their chasing each other and jumping over the gravestones of their ancient ancestors in a bizarre game of leapfrog.

Eventually Marjánka came to the U.S., was the first woman to earn a Ph.D. in divinity from Harvard, and became a Lutheran pastor. When that came to an end, she became a professor of religion at Duke University and later at Miami University in Ohio. Finally she retired and settled in a suburb of Chicago.

It was then that she and I connected. She became

my one Czech-speaking friend. She retained some of her professor-like behaviors, interrupting me in the middle of my Czech conversations whenever she found my grammar to be incorrect. This used to irritate me, but now I'm grateful. I think my Czech is a little better because of her punctiliousness.

Eva Lutovsky

My other friend who had lived in Prague during the war was Eva Lutovsky. We had the same Czech-American attorney, and we met in his waiting room. She insisted that she had gone to the same gymnasium in Prague as my brother Charlie, and that they rode the tram to school together every morning. Well, perhaps.

Eva's mother, Mrs. Hana Malková, was secretary to the puppet president of the Czech Protectorate, Emil Hácha. During the day, she took Hácha's dictation, filed his papers and documents, and served ersatz coffee to his visitors. At night she sheltered people who were being hounded by the Gestapo in her small suburban house outside of Prague. She was part of something like an "underground railroad" that saved the lives of many Jews and resistance fighters.

Eva described one event to me that occurred near the end of the war, in 1945. German troops were withdrawing westward, fleeing the Russian armies that were moving toward Berlin. Civilians, who had been encouraged by the German government to go east and occupy lands and homes abandoned by Poles, Croatians, and other Slavs while Germany was winning the war, were now fleeing the Russians and adding to the chaos.

On this occasion, Eva and her mother were in their home. Hiding in a back room under a pile of bedding was a young Jewish girl. A knock on the door. A German officer introduced himself, saying that his task was to scout out possible sites to house "our refugees" – the Germans fleeing back toward Germany. He said, looking around, "This house seems like a real possibility for us."

Mrs. Malková led him into her living room, saying she would prepare the house for his inspection, adding, "There is one problem that you will notice." While he waited, she rushed to Eva's room, told her to get in bed quickly, and to "act crazy" if anyone approached her room. Then, as she led the German officer down the hall, Eva started to scream: "Witch! Villain! Monster! Stay away!" and making dreadful noises. Mrs. Malková said to the officer with an embarrassed look, "This is the problem I was referring to, Sir. My daughter has serious psychiatric difficulties, and at this time I can't get any help for her."

The German officer said, "No, I see. This house would not be appropriate for our people. But there is a book in your living room bookcase that greatly interests me. It is the third edition of a particular biography of the poet Schiller that I have been seeking for some time. I wonder if I could borrow it for a few days."

It turned out that this particular officer, not at all a warrior by inclination, had been a professor of literature before the war, and that his interest in the Schiller biography was far greater than any willingness to look further into Eva's psychiatric problems. Mrs. Malková responded to his request by saying that he should keep the book as a memento of his sympathy toward her unhappy situation. He left quickly, carrying the Schiller book with profound devotion, like a sacrament. Eva, her mother, and their Jewish guest – who left later that night – were saved.

Later, Eva and her mother hid another young woman, Heda Kaufmanová, who worked with the Czech underground. Eva gave me a copy of Heda's memoir in typed manuscript form. It tells of narrow escapes, of heartbreaking executions, of messages sent back and forth in baskets of dirty laundry to and from prison. Heda survived the war in the home of Eva and her mother. After Eva escaped from the country when the Czech Communists established a different kind of totalitarian power, Heda stayed on and cared for Eva's mother until Hana Malková's death some years later. Mrs. Malková has been honored as one of the "Righteous Gentiles" by Yad Vashem.

CHAPTER 25

VINALHAVEN

We led a full life in Chicago, rich with family, friends, journalism, poetry, and politics. But there was a gap in our life experience that we needed to fill.

Ever since he was a baby, Mark's family had spent their summers on Peaks Island, an unspoiled spot off the coast of Portland, Maine. Mark's early poems tell about fishermen, ball games, the one soda fountain, Sunday dinners. Peaks Island personified freedom for him. When he brought me there, I fell in love with it as well. It was the ocean that drew me, having come from a country without a seacoast.

We decided to scout for our own Maine island. We explored Deer Isle; the Cranberry Islands, way up north; and Monhegan, the home of the painters Andrew and Jamie Wyeth. At the time, one could approach Monhegan only with the mail carrier, in an open boat that rocked perilously back and forth. The wind was ferocious as we approached the landing. My neighbor, holding on to the railing for dear life, laughed as he looked at me and asked, "Who does your hair?"

Our Final Choice

Our final choice was Vinalhaven, and we started to go there for summers in the early 1970s. It was reached by ferry from the town of Rockland. In those days before most cars were air-conditioned, we would wait impatiently in the Rockland ferry line, sitting in our hot car with two girls and a large Airedale dog named Barney in the back, having driven for three days from the Midwest. You really had to want to come, to take this trip.

The ferry loaded cars and passengers and took off for its hour-and-a-half ride to another world. Along the way we saw lobster boats, pleasure boats of all kinds, and, above all, the broad expanse of the sea itself. With luck, we might spot a family of seals or catch a fleeting glimpse of dolphins dancing in the rolling waves. And always the salty smell of the sea. There was the cawing of the seagulls and, periodically, the loud hooting of the horn of the ferry, which left Barney shaking in the back of the car.

A Village from Another Time

The trip ended at the landing of a small village where time seemed to have stopped in the 1940s. There was a grocery store, a library, and a post office. The social occasion of the day was the noon arrival of the mail by ferry, with the townspeople visiting in front of the post office while they waited. There was a hardware store with several odd chairs arranged in front to accommodate the town's old men, who gathered for a social time of their own in the early afternoon. There they sat, smoking, gossiping, watching the scene.

Fishermen and Artists

The chief industry of the island was lobstering, but there were also many artists. The pop-artist Robert Indiana bought a house downtown, remodeled it into a work studio and museum, and made it his year-round home. He once stopped at our house to evaluate our view. He approved.

The islanders were proud and kept to themselves. Everyone born on the island was called an islander. All the rest – people who came to retire on the island, summer visitors, including those who owned the fancy homes, known as "cottages," on the far end of the island – were "from away." We were "from away." The summer folk were generally tolerated. After all, they brought in a considerable part of the island's income and employed the carpenters, plumbers, and electricians necessary to keep the summer homes in good repair.

We Buy a House

We rented different cabins over three years. On the last day of our third visit, we took a goodbye ride around the town and stopped at a modest house with a breathtaking view of the bay and a sign in front: "For Sale." Tires and cartons of all sorts were scattered in front. Mark turned to me and said, "Anna, I bet we can afford this."

"No, No, Daddy!" screamed the girls from the back of the car. They were afraid that they would have to vacation amid tires, discarded cans and broken cartons.

The house was on Dogtown Road, a typical Vinalhaven street name. We hired people to clean the place up, knock down the outhouse, add a bathroom. Each year we gave ourselves a project: fix the cabinets, buy new furniture, add a room. We loved our Vinalhaven house. We kept it filled with wild flowers; brought in stones, shells and pottery; hung sketches made by our artist friends. I sometimes thought of it as a distant relative, perhaps an adopted seaside child of our house in Prague. Both houses were warm and welcoming.

For the next 30 years or so, we came back, at first with our daughters, then by ourselves, and always with our dog. We made friends among our neighbors – some "from away," a few islanders. Two or three became close friends.

Natural Wonders

It was the natural setting of the island that we thought of all winter and rushed to re-visit every possible summer. We waited for the bright early mornings, when only the twittering of what Mark called his "morning birds" broke the silence. We often took the girls swimming in the nearby quarry, which had been formed by mining granite to make pillars for grand places in New York, Boston and Philadelphia. It was filled with soft, velvety fresh water, much warmer than the sea. I'd swim across, constantly looking over my shoulder. There would be

Julie paddling after me, as island children jumped into the water from high rocks screaming warrior yells.

Lane's Island

Most of all, we looked forward to our visits to Lane's Island, a large protected expanse of wild moor. There were only two houses that were "grandfathered" in when the preserve was established. Greeted by the smell of wild rose and bayberry, we followed a path that led to the rocky shore. In early summer there were raspberries growing in spots, to be followed later by blueberries and blackberries. We climbed up and down, pushing aside the thick undergrowth. Sometimes the roses were so tall that we lost sight of Barney, and had to listen for the jingling of his tags to know where he was.

Finally – the rocky coast itself and the wide open ocean. We would spend hours on the rocks, watching the boats, the seagulls, listening for the rhythm of the waves while, in our early years there, the girls collected starfish, rocks, shells, and crabs at low tide. On wild days, the waves would rush up high and the surf would crash into the rocks below, thrilling us all.

Driving back home at the end of the summer was difficult, but it served its purpose. It prepared us for a different time of the year, fall in Chicago.

CHAPTER 26

ANOTHER MASARYK ENCOUNTER

I think it was in 1980 that I learned that Anna Masaryková, Herbert Masaryk's daughter, was visiting the United States. I was thrilled. I decided that I must try somehow to meet her, if only to touch, once more, the precious connection between my family and the Masaryks.

The connection between our families began long before I was born, well before World War I, when the Czechs were part of the Austro-Hungarian Empire. That was when my grandmother, Anna Nessy, met her nearby neighbor, Charlotte Garrigue Masaryk, wife of the future founder of Czechoslovakia, Thomas Garrigue Masaryk. Perhaps the two women connected at a political meeting or on a protest march. My mother was not clear about the specifics. But she was quite certain about her own close friendship from childhood with the couple's two daughters, Alice and Olga, and about my father's friendship with their first son, the painter Herbert Masaryk.

The next generation enters the story with Herbert's daughters, Anna and Herberta, and with Alice agreeing to be my godmother. Alice was probably godmother to other children as well, but she took an interest in me and her friendship with my mother was tight. The visit to the U.S of Alice's niece Anna was big news. At that time, Czechoslovakia was in the grip of a Stalinist dictatorship. Anna was an art historian held in great esteem by art scholars and, she told me later, she received periodic invitations to lecture in Europe's art centers. Each time, she was denied an exit permit by the Czech government.

It was no wonder that they were so controlling of Anna. As the granddaughter of the democratic first president of the country, a strong critic of Marxism, she expected nothing else. She had a very small apartment, and when the neighboring place became empty, she applied for permission, as required, to rent that apartment as well. She wanted to break down the wall between and thus enlarge her living space. No response.

Application and denial were repeated several times. Finally, she received a summons to report to the local police, who was also the landlord. As usual, she waited all day only to be told that some small detail was wrong or missing in her application. She made the correction and applied again. Same result.

Eventually Anna was told she could rent the apartment, but that she should expect no help from government workers in obtaining needed supplies or conveying them to her third floor flat. She was used to such petty humiliation. Over time, she acquired the supplies herself and with help from friends carried heavy planks of wood up three flights of stairs. The project was eventually completed.

Why the Permission To Travel This Time?

That is why it was so surprising that she was finally coming to the United States. Why did she get permission this time, and not before? Had there been a special invitation? We didn't know. She told me later that when she received the needed permits to leave the country, she was ordered to keep politics out of all conversations, to keep her whereabouts in the United States secret, and to travel with only a minimal amount of money: minimal enough to humiliate her. That is why she had to travel, as she put it, "practically like a beggar woman." And one could be sure that she was watched.

Determined to find Anna while she was in the country, I called whatever contacts I had, primarily in New York. The response was always that she was somewhere else, or that she had just left. Finally, someone said, "I think she is now in Chicago. But she is probably about to leave." My source thought that Anna was likely to stay with a curator from the Art Institute of Chicago, and gave me that person's address and telephone number.

I called, no answer. But the address was not far from our house. Realizing that I was probably on a wild goose chase, I wrote a letter to Anna in Czech, explaining who I was and telling of my parents' connection to her family. That evening, Mark and I walked to the curator's building, slipped an envelope with the letter inside under the door of her apartment, and went back home.

A Special Day

The next morning, I was getting ready to go to work when the phone rang. It was Anna. Could we meet? I called my office, said I was sick, and spent the rest of the day with Anna Masaryková. We were alone. She spoke of her life under the Communists, talked with laughter about accomplishing the expansion of her apartment, and asked me about my life.

Anna told me that the goal of her trip was to move the remains of her Aunt Alice, my godmother, from the Bohemian National Cemetery in Chicago to Lány, the presidential retreat near Prague where her father and her uncle Jan are buried. This was probably why the Czech government allowed her to travel to the U.S. Nothing political, nothing public, just family concerns. Mark joined us for dinner, and then we walked her back to the curator's home. She left Chicago the next day.

We saw Anna once more in Prague, with her sister Herberta, but that meeting did not have the intimacy of the earlier time. I brought her a small painting by the Czech artist Mánes that my father had loved. I knew he would have approved of my doing this.

CHAPTER 27

JULIA'S BLESSINGS

In her late eighties, my mother moved from her little home on my brother Paul's property in Yorktown Heights to live with us in Chicago. She was considerably diminished. I drove her to her weekly doctor appointments, and we managed to live together in this way much longer than Mark and I had feared. The sweetness of her nature remained – her laughter at silly jokes, her happiness when Kate or Julie came home from college, her delight in tossing a salad, her pleasure in our dog, her enjoyment of going shopping with me. And of course, both of us loved speaking in Czech.

We took Mother to concerts from time to time. Once, when George Szell was guest-conducting the Chicago Symphony, we thought she might like to see her old friend from Prague conduct again. She wanted to go backstage to greet him afterwards, and we did. He embraced her so hard that she disappeared completely from my line of vision. It was a special night.

Even when her memory began to fail her, Mother never lost her memory for music. She remembered the folk songs we sang together years ago, and she sang them now, in a cracked, quivering voice that I sometimes found heartbreaking.

She had devoted her life to hard work and accomplishment, so even now she needed to be occupied in some way that would be significant to her. I recalled her early skill at knitting. "Would you like to knit again?" I asked her.

"Yes," she answered, so we bought large knitting needles and lots of wool in many colors. Until she could no longer do it, she knitted little squares – red, blue, yellow, multi-colored – about one inch in size. After her death, someone suggested that I combine them and create an afghan. "That would be a mistake," I answered, "Their purpose is not utilitarian."

I still have a large basket full of small, colorful squares. Some can also be found in random places in my home: the sweater drawer, a suitcase, the tool box. When someone in the family moves, or finds a new job, when a baby is born, I send a little square in the mail. We call these squares "Julia's blessings." I brought two to Prague on my last visit there and stuffed them in a secret place.

Mother died peacefully in 1981, at the age of 92. She had so many friends in New York, we decided to hold a memorial service for her at the Jan Hus Church there that March. On that occasion, Mark delivered a final eulogy:

Anna, Kate, Julie and I think it is important to say something about the last decade of Mother's life... for Mother's life did not end when she left New York. It may be hard to realize, but she enjoyed a number of pleasures in her last decade, though her life gradually wound down to such an extent that she could not communicate through speech.

There were the many trips to the Fox River, where we sat and watched ducks bobbing and paddling, saw the great willows and the houses on the riverbank opposite, boats moving, kids fishing, reflections on the water. And Mother took pleasure in the patches of woods and the corn fields we passed along the way.

She enjoyed the letters, the holiday cards, and certainly the photos, tapes, and visits too… And when she finally needed 24-hour care and moved to a nursing home, there was a staff there that not only cared for Mother, but loved her – at least partly because the sweetness of her nature caused that love to bloom in them. The director of nursing said, "Julia was special to us. She couldn't communicate with us often, but when she did, there was a radiance about her."

And this brings me to a gift that this very old woman gave without ever knowing to all who were lucky enough to come into contact with her throughout her life – perhaps especially in her last years.

Mother showed without ever trying that it is possible to live without meanness, that it is possible to live without complaining, that goodness is a force in the world that sometimes changes people who come into contact with it.

For as age inevitably wore her down, these qualities – this gift – shone through more and more, until at the end I was reminded of a beautifully polished stone, small and shining, from which all else had been winnowed away."

CHAPTER 28

RETURN

My story ends as it began – with the house in Prague. I saw it again 40 years after we left it, when I revisited the city of my birth for the first time. It was 1983, and Mark and I went with my brother Paul. The dark Stalinist regime was still in power. There was a shabby sameness about the streets and the shops. All signs were uniform. The clothing stores announced, simply, "Men's Clothes," or "Women's Clothes." The few bookstores said only "Books," and the books inside – all of them – were exactly the same.

During our entire stay, a man with a bowler hat pulled over his face sat near the entrance to our hotel, reading a newspaper. To us he looked like a spy out of a German Expressionist film. People's faces had the same wary look. I saw few smiles, spoke with almost no one. But the city was still there, with its history and its memories. And, to our great joy, we were able to have an extended visit with Anna Masaryková and her sister Herberta.

Courtyard entrance

The House

Paul, Mark, and I walked everywhere, but first to our house, which stood undamaged, just as Paul and I remembered it. The shop nearby, where I had bought pencils, erasers, and notebooks for school, was still there, as were the gardens of Strahov, where I had played with my friends. We visited my old elementary school, and Mark snapped a picture of me standing at attention in front of the school, as if waiting for the whistle to summon me back into the classroom.

Before returning home, Mark and I walked once more from the Castle up the incline that led to our house. We entered the outer and inner courtyards and stood quietly at the front door for a last look. As I made my silent farewell, I heard, suddenly, noise behind the door. Someone was there!

I addressed the unknown person in Czech, gave my name, and asked him or her to open the door for a minute.

"It would mean so much to me," I said, "to look up and see the stairs I climbed every day as a child."

I was startled when a woman answered me angrily, "You get away from here. We know what you are and we don't want your kind here." What did she mean by "your kind?" American? Jewish? Hostile to the Party or the State? We walked quickly away.

Succeeding Residents

We learned from the Masaryk sisters that three residents had lived in the house after we left it in 1939. The first was a German general, during the war. When the democratic Czechoslovak Republic was restored following the defeat of Germany in 1945, its duration was short-lived. Within three years the multi-party system was replaced by a Communist dictatorship. A cabinet member of the new Stalinist regime was the second resident.

The third was Hana Benešová, the widow of Czechoslovakia's second president, Edvard Beneš. A committed democrat and close friend of Thomas Masaryk, the country's first president, Beneš had helplessly witnessed the Munich Agreement and the German occupation of the entire country that followed. He died soon after.

When the Communists came to power in 1948, following the brief postwar semi-democratic interlude, they needed a suitable location for Beneš's widow. They knew she was loved by the Czech people and therefore had to be treated with respect. The regime chose our house, perhaps, because it was up to appropriate standards, and also because it was near government buildings from which the secret police could monitor her and her visitors. The woman who spoke so rudely to me was probably part of the surveillance.

Mrs. Benešová lived in the house until her death, some 20 years after she moved there. My mother, who knew and honored Mrs. Benešová, was happy to learn that it was she who occupied the house. A terracotta relief of the face and upper body of the president's widow is now affixed to the street side of the house. It faces a life-size sculpture of her husband, which stands directly across the street.

The Velvet Revolution

Things changed dramatically in 1989, with the defeat of the Communist regime. Farmers, workers, and students crowded into Prague's Wenceslas Square in what came to be known as the "Velvet Revolution." They demanded a new constitution and free elections. The name of Václav Havel, the persecuted and imprisoned leader of dissident writers and intellectuals, was heard over and over from the crowd. An election brought Havel to the presidency.

One-party Communist rule in Czechoslovakia was over, and the long process of restoring the rule of law and freedom of expression had begun. From Chicago, we followed these events with excitement and happiness. My brothers' and my one regret was that our mother, who had died in 1981, could not know about these wonderful developments.

Soon after Czechoslovakia became, once again, a

multi-party democratic state, we learned that it was possible for Czech citizens to reclaim property that had been taken from them by either the Germans or the Communists. At the time, the city of Prague claimed ownership of our house, having seized it under the Communist regime for "non-payment of taxes by the owner." The owner at the time of the seizure was our widowed mother, who had neither been informed that the house had been returned to the family at the end of World War II, nor been told that she owed taxes on it.

Our Two Lawyers

My brothers and I decided to sue the city of Prague for the return of the house to us, as the lawful heirs of our parents. Paul had double citizenship, both American and Czech, so he was eligible to sue in the Czech courts. We were referred to an excellent Prague lawyer, Vladimir Jablonsky, who specialized

Attorney Jablonsky, Paul, and Anna conferring in Prague

in what was called "restitution issues." He sued the city of Prague on Paul's behalf. Later we found a Chicago lawyer, Joseph Vosicky Jr., who could practice in both Prague and Chicago. He covered the American side of the proceedings, kept us closely informed about developments in Prague, and became a good friend.

What followed was a decade of petitions, hearings, and appearances in various courts and before various judges. Mark and I thought all this activity was a wonderful adventure, an opportunity to go back to Prague several more times, and to observe and learn about the changes happening in Czech society. With regard to any possible success of the lawsuit, we were skeptics.

But then, in 2002, a surprising event. The woman judge who had been hostile to our case all along suddenly went on pregnancy leave, and the case was taken over by another judge – her husband. Much to our delight, he found in our favor, and we won the case. The house belonged once more to the Baecher family.

Charles and Anna celebrating the news from Prague

Reunion

To celebrate, we decided to take another trip back to Prague, and bring along as many of our family members as we could. At the time, Mark had retired from his full-time work at Rotary International, but he was still teaching. I had spent years directing an organization that serves blind students and adults. We were engaged in the cultural life of Chicago, and were exploring the offerings of the Lincoln Park Village, which helps adults to remain in their homes instead of retiring elsewhere. Now we terminated all of those activities and focused on planning our trip to Prague.

The oldest of us, my brother Charles, was ailing and could not join us, nor could our daughter Kate. My brother Paul brought his son Tom, daughter Susan, and his grandchildren, Anjuli and Sebastian. Mark and I brought our second daughter, Julie, her husband, Charlie, and their two sons, Alex and Ryan. We were a delegation from the past and from the future.

Mark and Julie in Prague

This time no one stopped us from walking into the house. The beautiful parquet floors throughout the first floor were badly damaged, the walls scarred. All the appliances in the kitchen and bathrooms had been removed. But the rooms were still intact. The music room – that most beautiful room where Thomas Masaryk, Albert Schweitzer, and Josef Suk had once visited, and where, as a child, I had crouched in the corner to listen to my mother practice and sing – was still there.

We stood together at the bay window, looking down at the red roofs of *Malá Strana*, the orchards of Strahov, and the historic city below, with its broad vista of bridges, gardens, and church spires. We walked through all the rooms, and I made my way to the kitchen, where I stood for a while and sent a silent kiss to Miss Cook, long gone.

A few weeks after we returned home, Paul called me from Florida. "Anna, two architects have gone over the house. Restoring it would be very expensive." He quoted an unbelievable figure. "The lawyer thinks we should sell it."

"Alright," I answered, "But wouldn't it be lovely for us to keep one of those little apartments for family vacations?" He called right back with an answer.

"No, we'd have to sell the house as a whole." After a while, I agreed.

We hung up, and I sat quietly, with my head in my hands. Another goodbye. After all, I argued with myself, we fought for the house to correct an injustice, not to return and live in Prague once more. When would I stop believing that fairy tales come true? Still, it hurt a bit.

Mark's Illness

In the meantime, we had other concerns, more important. We had known for some time that Mark had developed leukemia, but now it seemed to be in a new stage. Back in Chicago, he continued to teach and to write, but the trips to the hospital grew more frequent.

Mark taught his poetry workshop as long as he could, and he finished his last poem in the hospital, just before he died June 30, 2008. I think of him every day. I will always cherish our life together. In 2012, the Louisiana State University Press published his posthumous book, *The Theater of Memory: New and Selected Poems of Mark Perlberg.*

The Last Return

In the fall of 2012, I made my final return to Prague, this time with our first-born daughter, Kate. I showed her all I could of Prague, places I remembered and loved. But the house was our most important destination. It was undergoing extensive restoration, we were told, all veiled in secrecy. Our lawyer, Mr. Jablonsky, contacted the architect in charge, who invited us to visit the site. He picked us up at the Hotel Kampa and drove us to the house.

Kate and I walked from the arcaded street through the huge wooden doors into the outer courtyard, holding hands. The restoration of this courtyard was completed, and it was beautiful. This was where Father's experimental Tatra car was kept; in earlier times this may have been where carriages were housed. Moving toward the house itself, we walked through another, smaller door into the large inner courtyard.

We put on protective jackets and helmets and walked cautiously on wooden planks that formed a rickety narrow path leading to the front door of the house. We were astonished to see several people bending down, carefully digging and sifting through dirt and rubble. The architect told us that they were archaeologists, searching for artifacts from much earlier times. The house was many centuries old, he said, many more, perhaps, than had been originally thought.

His story stirred a memory. As a girl, I had been told that this house had been home to one of the Protestant nobles who were executed after their defeat by the Hapsburg forces at the battle of White Mountain in 1620, during the 30 Years' War. Now, he said, some artifacts had been found in the courtyard and in the house itself that seemed to confirm this story, and might even date back much earlier. Proof was still far off. In the meantime, the digging, the caution, and the intense protection went on.

But now the home itself. We entered through the frosted glass and iron door and made our way up the stairway to the front hall, with its large fireplace. Plastic sheeting barred entrance to many rooms. There was scaffolding everywhere. We walked up the centrally-located oak staircase to the second floor, passing oval art nouveau windows as we climbed.

The entrance to the second floor rooms was locked, but we could look through the glass upper panes of the door to scan the empty space and imagine what had been there. This was where my brothers and I spent our earliest days. I pointed out to Kate where my bed stood, where I kept my books and toys, and where I had a special table for drawing and coloring, later for doing my homework.

Next we walked to the very top of the staircase where a door was, mercifully, not locked. We stepped out on a small balcony that jutted out from the roof. We saw, it seemed, the whole of my Prague world below: the red roofs, the gardens, the twisted little streets of the old city, the spires, the bridges, the grand river.

Then back down the stairs again. The music room was accessible. The Italian frescoes had been taken down from the ceiling; we were told that the frescoes of all the downstairs rooms were being restored before being reinstalled. I showed Kate where the couches had been, the armchairs, the pianos, the harps, the giant Christmas tree in December. And of course we stood once more in the big bay and looked out on the city below.

It was time to go. I knew I might never see the house again. It had stood for many centuries, *Anna and Kate say goodbye to the house* survived great and evil times, including two terrible wars. It had housed many families, including my own, sheltered an honored widow. In my thoughts, it was almost a living, breathing thing, a refuge for us in the past, and perhaps for others in the future. I had brought two of my mother's little knitted squares, her "blessings," with me, and now I slipped them under a radiator in a silent embrace.

We took off our protective gear, returned it to the construction men, and thanked our kind guide. I took Kate's arm, and we walked through the inner and outer courtyards, through the tall, arched double doors to the cobblestoned street. We went to a nearby café and ordered *palačinky*, my favorite childhood treat – large, thin crepes rolled up with strawberry jam and topped with whipped cream. We added hot chocolate, because a cold October wind was blowing outside.

We sat in the café for a long time, saying little. In my thoughts, I felt the presence not only of my older daughter, but also of my early family. I imagined my mother's perfume lingering in the air. I heard Malva's rough laugh at some long-ago story. And I saw my father smile and raise his glass to all of us, both in the past and in the present. I looked up and saw my daughter watching me, wondering.

I thought once more of the house. It is part of me. Though I lived in it less than ten years, it gave me my Czech roots. I like to think that I carry its strong spirit within me. In turn, I know a part of me will always be there, in that house in Prague.

ACKNOWLEDGMENTS

I want to express special thanks to the following:

To *Prairie Schooner* at the University of Nebraska and its generous editor Hilda Raz, who was the first to publish a piece of mine, "Leaving," which appears in a somewhat altered form in this book; to John Marshall Law School's program for Czech law students and that school's annual trips to the Czech Republic, in which I have happily taken part; to Lincoln Park Village and its founding executive director, Dianne Campbell, who created a Chicago-based organization with programs that enable its adult members to maintain their lives in the Chicago community they love; to journalist Beth Finke and her memoir group, in whose company I wrote several pieces which appear in adapted form in this book; to the Newberry Library of Chicago and its programs and seminars; to Dick Simpson, who generously advised me on a number of critical start-up problems; to the Chicago Committee to Defend the Bill of Rights, its board and its president, Bob Clarke, for inviting me to join their never-ending pursuit of justice; to my agent, Joan Parker, who generously took a chance on a neophyte; to Joseph Vosicky, Jr., who shared, with great kindness, his extensive knowledge of the Czech community, both in Prague and in the U.S.; to Elmer Gertz, whose generous spirit and commitment to social justice made working with him a privilege; to my publisher and editor, Nancy Sayre, whose probing questions made me think and write deeper and better; to Michael Sayre, whose artistry made the book shine; to Charlotte Newfeld, who helped me solve a bird problem; to Marjánka Fousková, who helped keep the Czech language alive in me; to Andrea Swank, who was most insightful in her comments and who helped me with important format issues; to Mark Kipperman, who solved a music problem for me; to Scott Burgh, who located sources for me that clarified the relation between Edward R. Murrow and Paul Heller; to Helen Epstein, who inspired me with her book Where She Came From; to Marla Brodsky, whose expertise and friendship kept me going; to Caroline Heller, who first made me realize that lines of poetry could help save those who might otherwise perish; to my cousins, Ivan and Frank Backer, whose detailed and precise family trees surpass the giants of the Muir Woods; to Marie Winn, whose generous heart will always remind me of her mother; to Ben Altman, who defines friendship; to my son-in-law, Charlie Farwell, who, together with Julie, patiently and generously reproduced my manuscript and photographic materials so many times; to my grandson Joshua Friedberg, who helped me with a variety of technological problems and who taught me along the way; to his brother, Michael Friedberg, who invited me to meet and learn from his sixth- and eighth-grade students; to our daughters, Julie and Kate, both of whom read many sections of the manuscript and made significant and highly valuable suggestions; to my husband, Mark, who, among his many other gifts, showed me new ways of looking at the world; and to my parents, who showed me how to live in it.

CREDITS

Grateful acknowledgment is made to *Prairie Schooner*, a publication of the University of Nebraska – Lincoln, which published the author's essay entitled "Leaving" which appeared in Volume 84, Number 3, Fall 2010 edition, parts of which appear in adapted form in this book.

Family tree courtesy of Ivan and Frank Backer, illustrated by Michael Sayre

Except as noted below, all images are courtesy of the author.

Grateful acknowledgment is made for permission to reprint the image on page 16: "Praha Staroměstský orloj [Prague Astronomical Clock]" by Jack de Nijs, from Nationaal Archief, (CC-BY-SA-3.0)

Cover photographic credits:

Front cover: "German soldiers enter Prague 1939" author unknown, (CC-PD-Mark1.0-PD Old); "Statue of Liberty" author unknown, source www.pixabay.com, (CC0)

Back cover photograph of the author: ©Ben Altman, www.benaltman.net

BIBLIOGRAPHY

Albright, Madeleine Korbel, and William Woodward. *Prague Winter: A Personal Story of Remembrance and War, 1937-1948.* New York: Harper, an Imprint of HarperCollinsPublishers, 2012.

Backer, Ivan A. *My Train to Freedom: A Jewish Boy's Journey from Nazi Europe to a Life of Activism.* New York: Skyhorse Publishing, 2016.

Demetz, Peter. *Prague In Black And White; Scenes From the Life of a European City.* New York: Hill and Wang, 1997.

Epstein, Helen. *Children of the Holocaust: Conversations with Sons and Daughters of Survivors.* New York: Putnam, 1979.

Epstein, Helen. *Where She Came From: A Daughter's Search for Her Mother's History.* Boston: Little, Brown, 1997.

Heller, Caroline. *Reading Claudius: A Memoir in Two Parts.* New York: The Dial Press, 2015.

Heller, Paul. "A Concentration Camp Diary." *Midstream,* April, 1980.

Heller, Paul. "Autobiographic Sketches: The First Forty Years." Unpublished typescript, 1994.

Kaufmanová, Heda. "Leta 1938 – 1945. Vzpominky.
(The Years 1938 – 1945. Memories)." Unpublished manuscript,
written in 1947.

Klíma, Ivan. *My Crazy Century, A Memoir*, English Translation
from Czech by Craig Cravens. New York: Grove Press, 2013.

Korbel, Josef. *Twentieth-Century Czechoslovakia: The Meanings
of Its History*. New York: Columbia University Press, 1977.

Mitchell, Ruth Crawford. *Alice Garrigue Masaryk, 1879-1966*,
University Center for International Studies. Pittsburgh:
University of Pittsburgh Press, 1980.

Murrow, Edward R. and Bliss, Edward. *In Search of Light:
The Broadcasts of Edward R. Murrow 1938-1961*. New York:
Alfred A. Knopf, 1967.

Polak, Stanislav. *Charlotta Garrigue Masaryková* (in Czech).
Prague: Mladá Fronta, 1992.

Sperber, A. M. *Murrow. His Life And Times*. New York:
Fordham University Press, 1986.

INDEX

INDEX

ABOUT THE AUTHOR

Anna Nessy Perlberg was born in Prague in the late 1920s. She and her family escaped to New York just a few days after the Nazi invasion in 1939. Anna holds a Bachelor of Arts in History from Barnard College, a Master of Arts in History from Columbia University, and a Master of Social Work Administration from the University of Illinois. She has been published in several venues. Anna feels a connection with today's immigrant children and often speaks about her story to school groups. She and her late husband, the poet Mark Perlberg, settled in Chicago, where she resides.

If you would like to correspond with Anna or receive more stories of her Prague childhood and other exclusive content for free, please go to: www.goldenalleypress.com/anna-nessy-perlberg